# The Game Design Toolbox

This book presents 71 practical game design tools that readers can use to solve real-world game design problems. Written to be a "toolbox" for game designers, it offers a hands-on approach with clear and easy-to-use tools so that readers can quickly find the right solution to the problem they are facing.

This book is divided into six game design phases: ideation, exploration, commitment, problem solving, balancing, and tuning. Each category contains an array of relevant tools, and the accompanying indexes offer suggestions for tools to use for specific problems. Support Materials offer further teaching materials, exercises, and complementary FAQs.

Written to be a practical resource, this book will be a useful toolbox for junior and veteran game designers alike.

**Martin Annander** has worked with games since 2006 as a game designer, programmer, studio manager, and design director. He is currently an independent game designer and freelancer.

# The Game Design Toolbox

## Martin Annander

**CRC Press**
Taylor & Francis Group
Boca Raton  London  New York

CRC Press is an imprint of the
Taylor & Francis Group, an **informa** business

Designed cover image: Shutterstock

First edition published 2024
by CRC Press
2385 NW Executive Center Drive, Suite 320, Boca Raton, FL 33431

and by CRC Press
4 Park Square, Milton Park, Abingdon, Oxon, OX14 4RN

CRC Press is an imprint of Taylor & Francis Group, LLC

© 2024 Martin Annander

ISBN: 978-1-032-36587-9 (hbk)
ISBN: 978-1-032-36551-0 (pbk)
ISBN: 978-1-003-33275-6 (ebk)

DOI: 10.1201/9781003332756

Typeset in Minion
by codeMantra

Access the Support Materials: www.Routledge.com/9781032365879

# Contents

# Introduction

"We're sort of stuck. Can you suggest any good tools we can use?"

This question was asked in a game design workshop I once held. I had no good answer and didn't really know what a 'tool' was even supposed to be. Game designers are not carpenters, they're wizards, and wizards use wands. Right?

The question surely made me feel like a tool.

Later in the workshop, something I covered happened to fit the bill for what a 'tool' was supposed to be and the workshop attendees could bring it with them with some sense of satisfaction (and my relief).

The tool in question was something I had used plenty of times to find inspiration when none was to be found and something they could make good use of in the workshop and hopefully in their future as well.

But after the workshop, I kept coming back to that question. *Can you suggest any good tools we can use?*

I felt that how we actually do our game design seemed loose, undefined, and deeply prone to subjectivity. Call it instinct, experience, or gut reaction—whatever you may—it's still just a magic wand by another name.

My conclusion was that magic wands are simply not good enough and that there has to be something more to our craft. Some bona fide professionalism that makes our jobs jobs and not witchcraft. Game design can't simply be to have opinions about games on a daily basis, and whatever comes out at the end is accidental or even incidental.

At the same time, back in the game design mines of my day job it was clear that our communication wasn't really working. Since we didn't have any standardized way of talking shop, there was a noticeable lack of common ground. Misunderstandings were the norm and seniority was the decision maker.

Is *Dark Souls* hard? Is *Battlefield V* fast paced? Is *Candy Crush Saga*'s gameplay strategic? Is *Monopoly* satirical? Should all first-person

DOI: 10.1201/9781003332756-1

shooters have sprinting? Does the *Mage Knight* board game have too many components?

You can answer those questions however you want, and you'll be right, because the answers are perfectly and undeniably subjective.

This was exacerbated by game design lacking any kind of established faculty language. The nature of entertainment makes the creative conversation itself subjective. As a consequence, game designers often swear by the holy law of winging it until it works and calling it something that fits or that they heard in a Game Developers Conference (GDC) talk once. Often, it's not phrased as an actual strategy until long after the fact.

The combination of this subjectivity and lack of common language means that we fall back on referring to other games. Other games become the only common ground we can sometimes agree on. But this is problematic. As our experiences of playing said games will be just as subjective as the design process that made them, it means we can only agree when we reach the most high-level conclusions possible. This means that FPS games must have sprinting, because all of the ones we have played recently do.

We may not look at this as a problem in our daily duties, but it is. If we can't talk about our craft objectively, things will invariably fall into the design by reference or design by committee traps, and we're doomed to repeat the same mistakes forever without acknowledging that they're mistakes. Common tools would help us talk about the execution of a game's design on its own terms and to establish a language informed by the game we are developing. The tangible playable product in front of us.

Game design is no mystery, and if we turn it into one, we're admitting that we have no clue what we're doing. This is why it really bothered me that I couldn't immediately and spontaneously answer that question about tools.

Not good enough.

Moving forward, armed with the aforementioned reasons—a need for practical tools and a lack of a common language—I started thinking about what the screwdrivers, hammers, and power tools of our craft actually are. Whenever I thought of something I wrote it into a document. Wherever I was, whatever I was doing, and whoever I was stealing it from.

This toolbox is the result.

It's filled with some of the hands-on tricks and weird exercises I've used through the years to solve different types of design problems or to find a new path ahead when I got stuck. Many have been stolen from designers who are much smarter than I am, whom I will give due credit where I can remember them. Others have become best practices out of habit.

Keep this toolbox with you, and when you need a screwdriver to tighten a loose game design screw, reach down, find the tool that fits, and get on with the job.

**Martin Annander**
*April, 2023*

# CHAPTER 1

# Game Design

A S A FRAMEWORK FOR the toolbox, we will use two informal templates just to have a working definition of what a game designer does for a living. This is not an attempt to define anything—it's merely the framework for the tools in this book.

- The first relates to what game design is and serves to separate everyday discussions about games from the job of a game designer. It does this by dividing the role of a game designer into four separate levels, somewhat like the experience levels in a role-playing game.

- The second presents six stages of game design and acts as chapters for all the tools that form the bulk of this book. Each stage is a distinct part of the design process, even if they are rarely treated that way in practical scheduled reality.

## GAME DESIGNER

The following tries to lay out the work and the responsibilities that come with game design in a practical way.

If you're making analog games—card games, board games, tabletop role-playing games, *etc.*—you're more likely to work alone or in a small team. In digital game design, teams vary greatly in size from solo developers to giant cross-disciplinary studios distributed across multiple teams all over the globe.

Team size changes the dynamic of the work, but it doesn't really change the work. It does lead to specialization, however. In a really big team, you

DOI: 10.1201/9781003332756-2

may be entirely focused on a very small part of the design puzzle and never touch the other parts. But for the sake of this framework, we'll look at game design holistically. Just remember that it won't always be your responsibility to do *everything*.

To make a game designer's duties easier to talk about, those duties have been divided into four levels of game design. As with experience levels in role-playing games you start at Level 1 and will increase your level by gaining experience.

What you need to be aware of is that you can easily achieve different levels in different kinds of game design, or even between different individual projects, or even parts of the same project.

If you reach Level 3 for one project, you may very well fall back to Level 1 for the next one because it's too different from the previous project or goes into details you're not as familiar with.

Many experienced digital game designers struggle to make analog games because their ideas of what works and what doesn't won't transfer over as readily as they may have thought. In effect, a Level 4 digital game designer may very well be a Level 1 analog designer, or vice versa.

Your level as a game designer is about what you're doing right now and isn't a linear progression toward an inevitable level cap.

## Level 0: Non-Designer

Anyone with no practical knowledge or even interest in games will be a Level 0 game designer. Every time someone is surprised to learn that not all board games have dice or thinks that gaming is the same thing as gambling, they're Level 0 designers.

This is usually because they are not interested and have never had a good reason to become interested. They may still "level up" to a higher level someday by playing and starting to have opinions about games, but chances are that they'll remain uninterested indefinitely.

This is fine, as long as there's an understanding that this person won't be contributing to the design of your game. Make this clear as soon as possible, so there's no misunderstanding.

## Level 1: Opinionated Designer

For the most part, this is all game design actually is: having opinions about games. You like the thing—you don't like the thing. You want to change it—you don't want to change it. You want a helicopter and three more decks of cards, faster movement, and more ammo; or you don't.

Games, just like other forms of entertainment, speak to us on an instinctual level. Even when you can't explain the whys or wherefores, you may still have both feelings and opinions. But **everyone** has these feelings and opinions. If this is all game design is allowed to be, everyone is doing it all the time.

When the tester says that the character moves too slowly, the IT manager thinks that the game looks too dark, or your kid wants to see a turtle character in your game, that's game design too—and it's at least as valuable as the feelings and opinions of any other Level 1 game designer. It doesn't matter whether your title says "designer" or not. At this level, you are still very much designing games on equal terms with everybody else.

So, if you, the titular game designer, remain at this level you won't help your team or your play testers. You'll just be another voice phrasing opinions. You must do something that no one else can do if you want to attain a higher level. You must take one step above having opinions.

Always remember that everyone with feelings and opinions is a Level 1 game designer.

## Level 2: Proven Designer

The first thing you must do to increase your game design level is to iterate your designs and use that iteration to validate all the opinions from Level 1. Not just your opinions—everyone's opinions.

There are three steps to this.

First, you must remember that the end product is what matters. Not your idea of the end product, and not your own opinions on what the team is delivering. **Validation is about iteration**. Coming up with cool ideas and watching them crash and burn as they hit reality. Every time this happens, you'll learn something new that you can bring to the rest of the team, and you'll mature as a game designer. If you stick stubbornly to whichever idea you had at the start, even against mounting evidence of your idea's problems, you're staying at Level 1.

Second, you must do your due diligence: researching game design subjects, playing similar games, reading what fans of similar games think on Reddit, in reviews, and so on, and expanding your vocabulary for both game design in general and the specific game you're making in particular. This is to stay on top of the conversation. When someone mentions something related to your game, you must be able to respond with a good answer, even if that answer is "I don't know yet."

Third, you must explore all the ideas that are coming up. There are four ways you can explore ideas, borrowed from Chris Hecker's excellent talk on advanced prototyping.

### Steal!

Before you do anything else, see if you can use someone else's exploration. Contrary to your gut reaction, however, avoid taking it from other games. Steal from math, from psychology, from history, from movies, from TV shows, from books, from a calligraphy class, from carpentry, and from everything, everywhere, and everyday life.

This is what artists do when they make mood boards. What anyone does when they type things into a Google Images search or post a link to an online video. It's the fastest and most efficient way to "prototype" an idea, since someone else will already have done this work for you.

### Pen and Paper

Make board game prototypes. Write short stories taking place in the game's fiction. Write player stories that describe the experience of playing the finished design. Make interactive mockups using paper. Draw stick figures. Use cards, random tables, and dice, to generate fake play sessions.

This is fast and efficient, and can be used to both ask and answer very specific questions about your game before the "real" game takes shape.

### Simulated Prototype

Grab your game engine or another game engine where you're comfortable making rapid prototypes, and then build something that fakes a prototype.

This is especially useful if you're already comfortable with some parts of your game design but not others. You can then make abstractions of the parts you already know and focus on the ones you don't.

For example, Nicholas Lovell talks about a "retention layer prototype" in his book, *The Pyramid of Game Design*. It's built to prototype the parts that are not the core gameplay in the game and represents the known parts of the gameplay in abstract form with a button that simply says Play and displays a short timer when pressed. Such a retention prototype never actually launches any gameplay. Instead, it's built to demonstrate the game's retention loop and how player engagement is maintained over time.

Doing this prevents you from getting stuck on details that don't actually matter yet.

*Prototype*
If none of the other ways work, go to the game itself and iterate. Just avoid iterating in the real proper game and give the neat features a wide berth. Remember that you're just dipping your toes—you're not here for a swim.

## Level 3: Experienced Designer

After painfully building and burning your creations you will have gained a much deeper understanding of the subjects involved. What's important is that you know how the game works and you know why certain decisions had to be made. Preferably with real concrete examples, but theoretical knowledge can be good enough while getting a complex system off the ground. Just make sure it doesn't remain theoretical forever. **In the end, the only thing that matters is the playable game**.

The knowledge you've built by now is the important part, because it turns you into the person to ask. It lets you answer the hows and wherefores with confidence, using examples, and not just by winging it or leaning on seniority.

At this point it's not about your confidence in yourself anymore—that's what Level 2 is for. At Level 3, it's about gaining trust with your team. It's about their confidence in you as their game designer and making you the person to ask when they need an answer about the game's design.

Truth be told, you'll still wing it sometimes, but that's where the trust comes in. You've seen where the pillars, facts, and prototypes have taken you, and you can surmise what the new inputs would lead to from there. When you communicate this to your team, they will respect it and be prepared to run with it. Not because it says "designer" on a plaque somewhere but because they genuinely trust your word for it by now.

When you've reached this level and gained the team's confidence it takes you one additional step above having opinions about games. Then you simply have to keep doing it. Both to build a better understanding for yourself and to maintain the team's trust.

## Level 4: Holistic Designer

The discussion on whether it was the elfdwarves or the horsepandas that invaded the Woodland Realm suddenly matters less when the Woodland Realm gets cut. As does the difference between 0.155 and 0.1551 start to have such a small impact that it's hardly worth the 2-hour weekly "Balance Meeting" anymore.

This is where a Level 4 designer is needed.

You're now so comfortable in your responsibilities that you can talk to the team and the team trusts you, but you've also understood that it's your job to make the hard decisions that make it possible to ship the game. Cutting the Woodland Realm; saying that we can now cancel the weekly Balance Meeting.

Level 4 is about stepping up, taking responsibility, and delivering the game. Looking at your project less as a creative free-for-all and more as a product that needs to be wrapped up and delivered.

This doesn't mean you're done with your responsibilities from the other levels. Far from it. It only means that you need to make increasingly hard decisions and get comfortable with both the largest and smallest pieces of the design puzzle at the same time.

Your perspective has to be holistic because it concerns the whole game and not just the parts. You see the forest, because you helped plant all the trees.

You must also be pragmatic, because you have the ultimate responsibility, and you don't defer hard decisions to other people. **You make the hard decisions**. Respectfully, of course, but you make them, and you take responsibility for them. If the thing you said would work doesn't work, you step up to accept responsibility, and then you say how to move forward.

You can still have opinions about games, like every Level 1 game designer. But you've also become the person who will get asked, "how do we solve this?" and you'll be able to provide a satisfying answer that fits with the game's vision, the team's comfort, the budget, and everything else that goes into a project.

As a Level 4 designer, you're working on the whole product—not "just" the game design.

## STAGES OF A GAME'S DESIGN

The tools you find in the rest of this book have been divided into six separate stages of game design. Each section goes into what you need to deliver from that stage.

For now, let's just look at what these stages are.

## Ideation

Ideation tools help you come up with and discuss ideas. It's mostly about conversation and organization, learning how to be constructive and collaborative, and to deliver something concrete at the end of the process.

It's the part of the process that should invite as many Level 1 designers as possible, from across your team, acquaintances, or the communities where you hang out.

During ideation, anything goes.

## Exploration

Exploration tools dig into how you communicate, iterate on, and validate all the stuff that comes out of ideation. Understanding that it's fine if experiments fail and that everything that happens should be evaluated based on its own merits and not on preconceptions. It's where you have to accept the responsibilities of a Level 2 designer.

Whenever you step back to Ideation, you're once more at Level 1. The reason this distinction is important is that being at Level 1 puts you on the same game design level as the aforementioned QA tester and IT manager.

Exploration is where design is made concrete—it's where you start really **working** with game design.

## Commitment

Commitment tools help you decide which lessons from Exploration to push forward and when to completely abandon Ideation. It's a tricky but completely fundamental step for a game's design. If you never commit, you'll never finish your game, regardless of whether that game is a fun spare time project or a giant multi-million-dollar enterprise.

It comes most easily to Level 4 designers, who have been through this rodeo before, but will usually require at least a Level 3 designer to get the team to trust the decisions being made.

Committing too early may force you to ideate and explore when you should be focused on finishing the game, but committing too late won't give you enough time to get acquainted with the game you are making.

## Problem Solving

Problem solving tools switch your attention to the concrete issues with the current playable version of your game: controls that don't feel great, features that fall short, or components that are too fiddly or imprecise. It can be any apparent problem with the game as it currently is.

It's strictly for Level 2+ designers. If you approach problem solving as a Level 1 designer, it turns into a guessing game and becomes an extended form of ideation and exploration process that can go on indefinitely.

Problem solving is about taking the last important steps toward a finalized design.

## Balancing

Balancing tools are here to let you make both broad and fine strokes that makes the game feel even nicer after the biggest problems have been solved. Tweaking numbers and thinking of how your content can be made to give the player the best user experience possible.

Interestingly, anyone can suggest things during balancing. Many Level 1 designers will contribute thoughts and suggestions, but you need Level 3 designers to receive, process, and handle this information. You also need Level 4 designer decision-making so that balancing doesn't go on forever.

You'll never feel completely done with balancing but must learn to contend with "good enough."

## Tuning

Tuning tools are the end station. The tweaks, changes, and clarifications that take your mostly finished game and removes the "mostly." When people talk about finishing something, this part is what they're talking about. It's sometimes referred to as the second 90% that you can only get to after finishing the first 90%.

It's important that Level 1 designers are not heeded at this point, and there's not a lot of room for Level 2 or even Level 3 designers either. It's strictly the domain of designers who have the credibility and authority to make hard decisions based on what's good for the game rather than what may sound good for a specific part of it.

This is the hardest part, by far, but may also be the most important.

## MECHANICS, DYNAMICS, AESTHETICS (MDA)

*MDA: A Formal Approach to Game Design and Game Research* is a paper co-written by Robin Hunicke, Marc LeBlanc, and Robert Zubek. It presents a framework for game design where the player's and the designer's perspectives can be handily separated.

The paper is just a five-page read that you should allow yourself in full at some point. For now, accept that games can be divided into Mechanics, Dynamics, and Aesthetics. (We will return to this at the very end of production, for different reasons.)

**Mechanics** are the data, components, and algorithms, **Dynamics** encompass the interactive behavior of the mechanics, and **Aesthetics** describe the emotions you want the player to feel while playing the game. There is more to it in the paper, of course, but this is where it gets interesting.

A game designer often starts from the mechanics and digs into the dynamics from there. There will be a concept of esthetics too, for many designers period particularly for those that apply their minds to theme before they look into gameplay. But even then, a designer has to consider the hows and whys before going too deep into the Aesthetics.

The player, on the other hand, will be experiencing the game from the opposite end. They will look at the aesthetics first, gradually immerse themselves in the dynamics, and may eventually learn about the mechanics underlying the dynamics if they become big fans of the game.

This is an incredibly important change in perspective that you must be aware of as a game designer. Players who don't understand your mechanics aren't "stupid" or "idiots," as you may want to call them; they're merely coming at it from another angle and have never been introduced to your design intentions.

Changing your perspective is of course extremely hard, but it's absolutely necessary, and some of the tools in this book will use the implications of the MDA framework as a reference for this specific reason.

## MECHANICS

PRESSING SHIFT OR LEFT
STICK BUTTON TRIGGERS "SPRINT,"
MOVING YOU FOUR TIMES FASTER.

## DYNAMICS

WHEN I GET HURT, I CAN SPRINT
TO COVER TO SAFELY REGENERATE
HEALTH WITHOUT GETTING SHOT.

## AESTHETICS

CAPTAIN SOLDIER RUNS AS FAST
AS POSSIBLE INTO COVER, WHEN
THE MACHINE GUN OPENS FIRE!

## LOOPS AND HOOPS

Something we often refer to in game design is the loop. There are many different loops, however; so let's clarify what we tend to talk about with a bit of vocabulary that will be useful when you read the tools.

The loops described here are there to make the game fun to play (gameplay loop), keep you playing (compulsion loop), and keep you coming back for more (retention loop).

### Gameplay Loop

The types of choices and interactions the player is expected to do over and over again can be referred to as a gameplay loop. How interesting this loop is will often be the responsibility of a game designer.

Many game designs start by settling on a solid gameplay loop and then expanding on it.

- **Objects**: things that exist to be interacted with. Weapons, tools, cards, dice, flames, game boards, *etc.*

- **Actors**: things that are performing actions using objects. Players, characters, artificial intelligence, random generators, and so on.

- **Actions**: things that actors do. The verbs of the game.

- **Events**: things that happen based on actions. The outcome of actions.

### GAMEPLAY LOOP

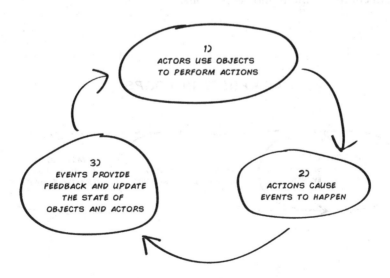

1) ACTORS USE OBJECTS TO PERFORM ACTIONS

2) ACTIONS CAUSE EVENTS TO HAPPEN

3) EVENTS PROVIDE FEEDBACK AND UPDATE THE STATE OF OBJECTS AND ACTORS

Compulsion Loop

"By itself, the story wouldn't make much of a novel," said Erik Wolpaw and Kim Swift about their game *Portal*; and "The gameplay on its own would be dry."

What many game designers talk about when they talk about loops is the engine that drives player engagement and not just the gameplay loop.

Whether a drip-feed of increasing rewards is the heart of this mechanism, or progression of one kind or another, this loop is often divided into three separate loops that can be referred to in slightly different ways.

First, you have the **Micro Loop** or second-to-second engagement: playing a card, switching guns, jumping a gap, spotting an obstacle, or finishing your turn. This is often the same as the gameplay loop mentioned before, but it's relevant to think of it also in terms of compulsion, since a game's design is rarely stronger than its staying power and a repetitive gameplay loop on its own may lose appeal over time.

Second, the **Macro Loop** or minute-to-minute engagement: completing an objective or challenge, defeating an enemy, or executing a nice card combo. "Just one more turn" in Civilization, or "just one more match" in a fighting game. Whatever it is that makes us want to dive back into the micro loop.

Third, the **Meta Loop** or hour-to-hour engagement. This is where a game's narrative is revealed, where you win a match, where system mastery may develop, and player engagement hooks into a higher level of compulsion. This is what's keeping you engaged both in very long single sessions and in chunks of many shorter sessions.

**COMPULSION LOOPS**

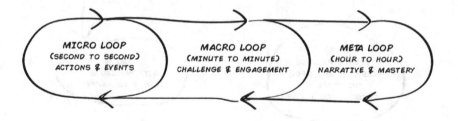

Retention Loop

Some loops are designed to make players come back to the game after leaving it, over and over and over again, particularly in games where the designers want players to spend lots of time (and/or money).

This holds equally true for subscription-based games, free-to-play games with in-game purchases, and also trading card games and collectible card games in the analog game space. But it's not just about money either. Any single-player game with a massive 100-hour campaign or scenario-based wargame with 20+ unique scenarios requires some kind of incentive for players to come back.

A solid retention loop needs opportunities for players to leave the game naturally and to ease back into it with as little friction as possible.

The first stage of retention is **engagement**. Get the player involved with playing the game. This is where the Gameplay Loop and Compulsion Loop are doing the heavy lifting, and not something the retention loop handles.

Second, you have **progression**. Whether by winning matches, unlocking rewards, or continuing through a monthly battle pass, this is a central part of retention. Many game designs rely on content additions for this stage: new card packs, new game modes, and additional levels—**more** of something.

Thirdly, there needs to be a **return call**. Something that schedules the player to come back after wrapping up. Once again, in Nicholas Lovell's book *The Pyramid of Game Design*, the author refers to having a natural **on-ramp** for players to get back into the game, but also a natural **off-ramp** for them to easily leave when they are done playing.

Finally, many games with successful retention provide **community** beyond the game. Not just actual online communities discussing lore and strategies, but also additional interfaces, for example *Destiny 2* and its companion app where you can manipulate how your gear is without having to launch the game. Prerelease tournaments for new *Magic: The Gathering* cards serve the same purpose: making fans keep other fans playing.

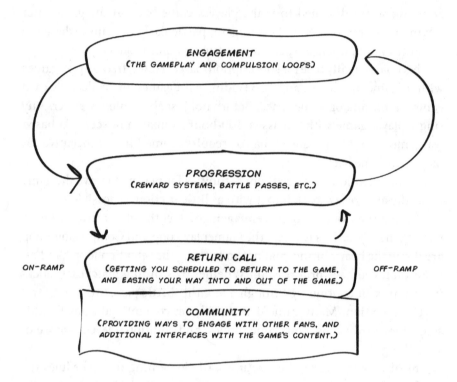

RETENTION LOOP

ENGAGEMENT
(THE GAMEPLAY AND COMPULSION LOOPS)

PROGRESSION
(REWARD SYSTEMS, BATTLE PASSES, ETC.)

ON-RAMP

RETURN CALL
(GETTING YOU SCHEDULED TO RETURN TO THE GAME,
AND EASING YOUR WAY INTO AND OUT OF THE GAME.)

OFF-RAMP

COMMUNITY
(PROVIDING WAYS TO ENGAGE WITH OTHER FANS, AND
ADDITIONAL INTERFACES WITH THE GAME'S CONTENT.)

## EMBRACING SUBJECTIVITY

Consider the rhetorical questions asked in the introduction. Is *Dark Souls* hard? Is *Battlefield V* fast paced? Is *Candy Crush Saga*'s gameplay strategic? Is *Monopoly* satirizing capitalism? Should all first-person shooters have sprinting? Does the *Mage Knight* board game have too many components?

Yes and no—both at once.

While brainstorming game ideas and talking about games we enjoy, always observe your use of language and your own biases so you can take this subjectivity into account. If not, you will run into the most common of all issues in game design—subjective discourse attempting to reach objective conclusions.

The first issue comes from talking about what we think is **fun**. This is partly because fun isn't always a goal and partly because fun is unrepentantly subjective. Many players enjoy competition, for example, and play hours upon hours of player versus player games. Others prefer to cooperate or play solitaire. Arguing on the basis of what's fun is therefore useless. Not because someone is wrong, but because everyone will be subjectively right.

Secondly, the mainstream consensus on what's commonly seen as **good** or **bad** can be discerned from the vocal voices in comments sections. But just as with fun, using a game's perceived goodness as an argument makes for a useless argument, especially if you are using it to evaluate a tiny part of a game and even worse if you're using it as an example for a solution in your own design.

Imagine that you're talking about the player needing a solution to a problem, and you're looking at games that have solutions to said problem. In most conversations, you're more likely to use examples from games you think are fun or good (see above), and you will then pick mechanics from those games to solve your problem—even if the problem is completely unrelated. This can be called **feature prejudice**, where you make the mistake of equating a dynamic with one of its underlying mechanics, and this is a direct consequence of our lack of respect for the subjectivity in our craft.

## Embracing Subjectivity in Practice

The following are some reminders you can use to embrace the subjective nature of game design. These can be much more useful than you may think.

- **Avoid referring to other games:** This is hard, because the games we all play are the only common ground we typically have. But once you have gone through ideation and exploration, and committed to your game, you will usually have a more established language for it.

- **Define a language around your own game**: Pillars, Features, Facts, and many of the other tools in the Commitment chapter are specifically tailored for this purpose.

- **Avoid saying what's fun or not fun**; what's good or bad. Instead, talk about the reasons you would want to use those words. Even better, talk about the takeaways you can make and where they tie into your own game.

- **Avoid borrowing individual mechanics** from games where they serve a wider dynamic. Just because you think a game is fun (or not) doesn't automatically validate a mechanic for your own personal use. There are often details in play that may not be immediately obvious.

- **Piggyback as little as possible** on other games, when you start your own project. Piggyback later—when you have more confidence in your idea. If you piggyback early, there's a risk that it becomes plagiarism instead, because you have replaced your own game's identity with that of the game you used to piggyback on.

- **Make no difference between games**: Whether played on a board, with a controller, touch screen, virtual reality headset, or with playing cards, there's a ton of overlap and cross-pollination between different types of games. Make use of the similarities—work around the differences.

- **Don't be vindictive**: If someone was against your idea, don't go against their idea as retaliation. This can be almost subconscious sometimes and not out of spite at all—just being human—so try to be aware of when you are about to shoot something down for the wrong reason.

- **Don't use "wrong"/"right"** when those words don't apply. In game design, as in so many creative crafts, there is rarely any objective way to be wrong or to be right. Try to motivate your arguments by merit instead, even if the only merit they have is that it's something you enjoy or something you prefer. Be honest when that is the case.

- **Don't die on hills**: Sometimes you just don't want to give up. This thing you find important is the most important thing ever and you'll gravitate back to it when it's not even relevant. Avoid this. There are no hills worth dying on.

## THE TOOLS

The rest of this book is the tools part of the toolbox.

Each tool has the same setup:

- A brief description that motivates why you should use it and talks about when it's most useful.

- A step-by-step guide, an example, or a checklist to follow when you use the tool. It varies widely between tools, but there's always some practical guideline available.

- An illustration that demonstrates how the tool looks like in use and how to make use of it, or just tries to make fun of it.

# CHAPTER 2

# Ideation

M ANY DESIGNERS THRIVE ON ideation. Coming up with crazy mechanics and clever solutions to theoretical problems. Having ideas at the speed of thought—maybe faster.

Ideas are fun and discussing them even more so. But there are some ways you can make the ideation process more constructive and a few essential principles you should keep in mind.

There are a number of things you need to achieve with ideation:

- A pared-down list of ideas that deserve to be explored, already scrutinized by yourself and any colleagues.

- Workable questions to validate in Exploration.

- A means to communicate what your ideas are about, to yourself and others.

- Ways to sell the best ideas to your team, if you have one.

DOI: 10.1201/9781003332756-3

## ASK FEWER QUESTIONS

Many tools in this section will tell you to ask questions. This makes it an odd thing to first state that you should ask fewer questions. So, let's get some context.

Imagine a brainstorming meeting or game design conversation. Everyone is talking about what the camera perspective should be. Maybe someone throws out the seemingly innocent question, "can we make it first-person?"

Our brains are our biggest enemies here. The brain doesn't listen to a question as a question; it often listens to a question as a suggestion.

Let's make it first-person, then. Let your mind spin its yarn from that and forget whatever perspective you had in mind before this seemingly—and intentionally—innocent question.

It also matters who asks the question. What if it's your lead, or even the company CEO; it easily takes on a different tone.

So, before you begin ideation in full, consider how you ask questions. It may even be a good idea to write things down before you say them, and then take a good look at what you wrote 5 minutes later. Chances are the things you wanted to say don't even need saying, because the conversation has moved on. Particularly if it was a question that would've taken things in a different direction.

Questions to (Maybe) Avoid in Ideation

- **Is it possible to do X?** No one, particularly developers, will ever admit that something isn't possible, making this a misleading question and not merely a veiled suggestion.

- **Can we make it X?** Same thing. Yes, we can, but that doesn't address whether we should or why.

- **Do you mean like X or like Y?** Introduces a false dichotomy. It could be that the real answer is Z, or the number 25. If you introduce binary selections on your own terms, you're forcing an answer that complies with your ideas.

- **Do you really like X?** A value-loaded question that implies that something is wrong with the suggested opinion and may force the person to rethink.

- **Do you like X? I really like X.** Risks replacing a person's own ideas with yours on the basis of an assumed mutual understanding.

- **Isn't this just X?/Isn't this exactly like X?/Do you mean like in X?** Nothing derails a conversation quite as much as unwanted or unneeded labeling, or what can be jokingly referred to as "reference tennis," where we bounce game titles between each other until someone names a game no one has played.

Questions to Ask Often in Ideation

- **Do you think that X also implies Y?** Allow the other person to verify what you're suggesting, or to extrapolate.

- **What if we also do X?/Can we try X, you think?** Again, defer extrapolation to the person with the suggestion.

## BRAINSTORM ON PAPER

Everyone files into the meeting room. There's an agenda, or there isn't (usually there isn't). As the meeting starts, there are 15 minutes of anecdotes delivered by that person who always delivers long-winded anecdotes. Then each discussion veers off into whatever the most vocal participant wants to talk about. For some reason, it's often the most recent gaming megahit. People who talk a lot tend to be the ones who are heard. But as has already been covered, everyone is a Level 1 game designer. Being vocal shouldn't be a criterion.

To give everyone a chance to be heard, and to get all the great ideas from people who prefer to stay quiet, brainstorming on paper is an effective tool.

If you're a vocal person, it'll often be tempting to talk about the notes you get or to talk over the whole process. But it's extremely important that you stay quiet throughout the process and let things take their time.

Brainstorming on paper can also be used as a means to gather feedback after a play test, so as not to contaminate the feedback with the opinions of the loudest voices.

There's also a reason this is the second tool in the book. When a new project gets off the ground, it's great to gather ideas from as many people as possible. It doesn't matter if the idea is completely unknown at this stage, or if you already know roughly what kind of project it's going to be. It's still extremely valuable to allow all Level 1 designers to take equal part in the initial ideation.

Brainstorming on Paper

1. Assign a moderator (doesn't have to be a game designer).

2. Collect possible topics for discussion through anonymous means. One sentence at most. Maybe, "Who is the antagonist?" or "What kinds of verbs do we want in our game?"

3. Gather the participants in a meeting room (physical or online).

4. Give everyone an individual piece of paper or digital equivalent, for notetaking.

5. Bring up one of the single-sentence topics for brainstorming. The moderator may elaborate on the topic, if needed. It's fine to ask questions at this stage—but only the moderator should answer, and it shouldn't bring up any creative topics for discussion.

6. Ask everyone to write their answer on their piece of paper. But no one is allowed to talk. Use an alarm clock, raised hands, pens put down, or another quiet means for everyone to signal that they are done with this stage.

7. Once done, pass the paper to the next person clockwise around the table and repeat the process for the same topic. This allows everyone to take their time, look at what other participants are thinking, and put it all in writing.

8. When you receive your own notes once more, so that each paper has done a full lap around the table, you may have an open discussion about what you've written, with everyone given a turn to speak or you may go back to #4, starting with a new piece of paper and a new topic.

9. The result of this process, once stages 4–8 have been repeated the desired number of times, is the sum of the group's ideas.

### BRAINSTORMING QUESTION:
### "WHAT GUNS SHOULD WE HAVE IN OUR GAME?"

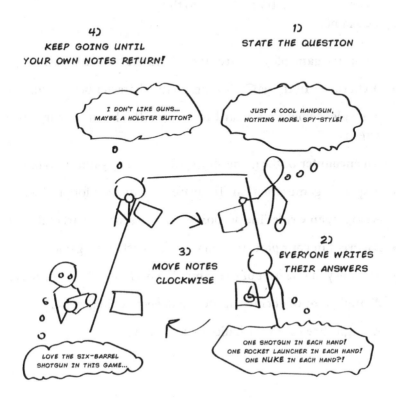

## ZOOM IN, ZOOM OUT

Sometimes you get stuck. Stuck discussing elements of the overarching plot in your game, or perhaps stuck talking about the same incrementally improved minor feature for hours.

These conversations can be valuable ways to ideate or explore, but it doesn't help your ideation to get stuck for too long on something that doesn't lead anywhere.

Many of the conversations we have in game development are simply fun to have, and even if we rationally know that we can't talk a game into existence it sometimes feels great to do so anyway.

What you can do to get unstuck is to invert the scope of the conversation. Getting stuck on small things, you zoom out to talk about a big thing. Getting stuck on big things, you zoom in to discuss a small thing.

Neither situation means that you permanently abandon the topic you got stuck on, but it may keep you—and your game's ideation—moving forward.

### Zooming

If you get stuck on one; try switching to the other.

Some examples:

- **A specific gameplay feature**: The system the feature is part of.
- **A character in the game**: The group the character belongs to.
- **A single element on a card or screen**: The layout of cards or the screen.
- **An encounter in the game**: The system used by game encounters.
- **A specific game situation**: The player's motivation for playing.
- **A single game rule**: The purpose of the rules for the part of the game.
- **An event in your plot**: The story for that part of the game.
- **The story in one part of the game**: The narrative of the entire game.
- **A single type of enemy**: The design of enemies in general.
- **A single dice roll**: Which dice to use in the game.

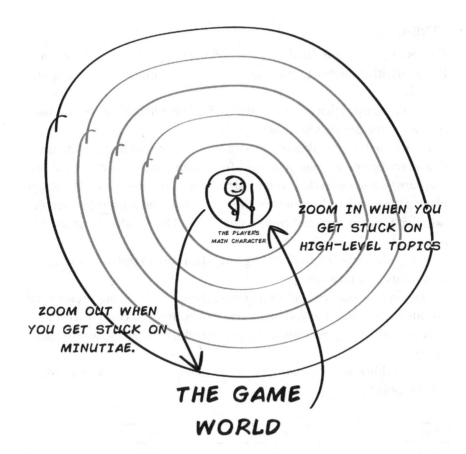

THE PLAYER'S
MAIN CHARACTER

ZOOM IN WHEN YOU
GET STUCK ON
HIGH-LEVEL TOPICS

ZOOM OUT WHEN
YOU GET STUCK ON
MINUTIAE.

THE GAME
WORLD

## VERBALIZE

Games are often simulated activities. Players or their avatars are doing things, whether jumping, shooting, conquering, talking, or something else entirely.

A verb is a word that expresses **action**. Verbs are in some ways the magic spells of game design. Our power words.

Because of this, it makes sense to start ideation by coming up with verbs that describe the actions you want from your game. Strictly speaking, there are two sets of actions you need to come up with—one for the player playing the game, and another for the avatar that represents the player. But skip that for now. Just let it come naturally (and from using other tools in this chapter).

It helps to visualize playing the game when you do this, and listing the verbs that come up as you go.

One exercise that may help is that you take out the most important verbs already at this stage and you map them to a button in a control scheme or by listing which components will represent which verb in an analog game design.

Try to think with a controller (or the components) in your hand, as early as possible.

| | | |
|---|---|---|
| Accept | Choose | Examine |
| Accuse | Climb | Exit |
| Acquire | Color | Explore |
| Assault | Create | Fall |
| Attack | Complete | Feed |
| Bake | Console | Fight |
| Become | Cry | Flee |
| Befriend | Dance | Fly |
| Bite | Destroy | Give |
| Blackmail | Die | Gossip |
| Break | Divide | Grow |
| Build | Draw | Harm |
| Burn | Drink | Hate |
| Buy | Drive | Hear |
| Catch | Eat | Hit |
| Change | Enter | Hold |

| Hope | Manage | Run |
|---|---|---|
| Hug | Modify | Sell |
| Imitate | Need | See |
| Improve | Negotiate | Seek |
| Intimidate | Notice | Shoot |
| Invent | Operate | Shop |
| Invest | Own | Sing |
| Jump | Paint | Sink |
| Jury-rig | Plan | Sleep |
| Journey | Promise | Solve |
| Kick | Quit | Spin |
| Kill | Read | Study |
| Kiss | Receive | Swim |
| Lead | Reduce | Taste |
| Learn | Replace | Tend |
| Lie | Rescue | Touch |
| Listen | Ride | Travel |
| Lose | Rotate | Win |

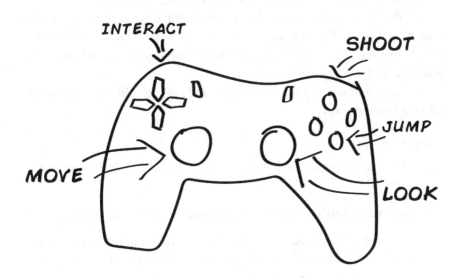

## SAY "YES, AND..."

Too often, our gut instinct is to shoot things down. To say "no, that's a bad idea," or to move on to some tangent. Our mode of discourse is often divisive or partisan: we're for or against things, or we read unintended passive-aggressive subtext into sentences that have no ulterior motives. Especially in online communication.

But there is a great middle ground that you can learn to utilize, and it's a concept from improvisational comedy: "yes, and..."

The basic idea is that you build something more on top of what was just said. If someone says, "maybe the elves did it?", and all you really want to do is blame it on the dwarfs instead, you don't do that—you keep building on top. You say, "yes, and the dwarfs were in on it too."

Positive reinforcement is a delicate process, however. There's a risk that your yes will still sound like a no, if you're not careful how you use it. "Yes, and then the dwarfs came in and took over" wouldn't be a very nice way to do it, for example, since it would replace what the previous person just said with your own idea.

Basically: the 'yes' accepts the previous statement as true, and the 'and' keeps building on top of it. When everyone in a meeting or design discussion uses this simple technique, you can have much more rewarding conversations and you will be able to brainstorm more effectively.

For the "yes, and..." to work, the statement it succeeds can't be too long or elaborate. If you need to listen to the whole history of the elves for 2 hours before you get to say your "yes," it becomes hard to know what you're actually saying yes to.

Stay brief and to the point in ideation, and regularly invite more people into the conversation.

Using "Yes, and..."

- Make single-sentence statements that are easy to build on and to accept.

- Listen carefully to what the other participants are suggesting.

- Respond by immediately saying "yes," even if you don't have the follow-up planned or if your gut says no. This is to teach yourself to be more positive toward other designers' suggestions.

- Say "and," then add your own constructive spin to what was just said.

- As an exercise, you can keep this going around the room until everyone has contributed something to the same idea.

WHAT IF WE'RE PLAYING RODENTS!
INTELLIGENT RODENTS PLAYING D&D
IN SOMEONE'S BASEMENT?

COMPARE THIS:

YUK! MUST IT BE RODENTS?
SERIOUSLY? RODENTS ARE DISGUSTING.

I THINK PLAYERS WILL LIKE
CROCODILES MORE.
LET'S GO WITH CROCODILES!

...TO THIS:

YES! AND THEY SQUEAL REAL LOUD AND
GNAW UP THE DICE IF THEY CRIT FAIL. HAHA!
WE CAN DO AWESOME THINGS WITH RODENTS.

YES, AND YOU CAN CUSTOMIZE
YOUR RODENT. FUR COLOR, TEETH LENGTH,
MAYBE SCARS?

## TRY IT

Games are nothing but the playable thing in your hand. But game designers in particular are fond of theoretical discussions about everything and nothing, all at once.

When you find yourself in such a discussion—particularly if it's the "wouldn't it be cool if"-kind—feel free to inject a suggestion to "try it!"

To "try it" is to take something directly to Exploration by building a prototype, finding another game that does a similar thing and playing it, or otherwise pushing forward into a practical representation of the specific idea. To avoid getting stuck in theoretical discussions and going straight to proving the idea's validity. Even if this is only done in isolated form.

This does three things: it acknowledges whether the idea has merit, it builds excitement to see how it works, and it forces you to think about all the hows and whys instead of leaving it at the ideas stage. If you **want it** to stay at the ideas stage, it also forces you to be honest about it.

Urging someone to "try it!" should be a spontaneously positive response and should never be used in an ironic or negative way. It should come from a place of genuine interest.

What it does is that it stops game design ideation from getting stuck in the stage where all we do is talk about possibilities. After all, having ideas will never make a game.

When to Say, "Try It!"

- "I have an idea I came up with that's…" Try it!

- "What if we take this feature and do this thing instead?" Try it!

- "This neat experiment could maybe have some interesting results…" Try it!

- "Not sure that's such a good idea…" Try it!

- "Never seen this before!" Try it!

- "Don't think we can do this in our engine…" Try it!

## SET A THEME

One of the oldest discussions in game design is whether designers should start from theme or from mechanics. It's a chicken-or-egg kind of causality dilemma, if we're honest about it. You do you. But starting from a theme can hold incredible merit, particularly when working with people who have very different sets of skills from your own. A theme may bridge the conversational gaps much faster than other types of overarching guidelines and they can help you get off the ground with the mechanical parts of your game.

"Theme" in game design is most often used to describe the context of the whole game. It's usually more than the literary theme that gets included. It's the whole range of literary elements, or a choice selection of them.

When you discuss the theme of a game it helps to widen the conversation to include the full range of literary elements. Some or all of them are what gets included when "theme" is discussed in game design anyway. So, make it part of your conversation.

Once you have established your theme, use it to inform your ideation. Use it to ask better questions and to find out what's important to explore.

Literary Elements Included in Game Design "Theme"

- **Characters**: who the characters in the game are, if there are characters. Note that a character doesn't have to be a person—it can be a spaceship, a horse, a house, a storm, or something else that reinforces the game's theme. Something the game can be about.

- **Narrative theme**: a subject or emotion, such as parenthood, survival, fanaticism, or redemption.

- **Setting**: where and when your game is taking place, as a backdrop or as explicit world building.

- **Plot**: the relationship between different events in the game's story, if there is one. In game design, a plot can also be generated by player activity.

- **Story**: the specific narrative that the game is designed to tell the player.

- **Conflict**: the central conflict of interest that pits the player's forces against the games, or players against players.

- **Perspective**: whose point of view is being portrayed or illustrated by the game.

- **Tone**: if it's heavy, light-hearted, critical, political, or something (anything) else.

- **Pace**: how fast the concept is. If it has the pacing of an action movie, or a drama, or a stage play, or something else entirely.

- **Style**: the way a theme is conveyed can be varied by the choice of words, game content, and what a player gets rewarded for doing. Think of the difference between adding a time penalty and giving you points for running over a pedestrian in a street racing game.

- **Narrative genre**: thriller, horror, comedy, tragedy or something else; whatever you may want.

## INVENT A MECHANIC

There are two ways you can fairly consistently come up with "new" mechanics to explore: by deriving them from existing game experiences, and by inventing them from theme, constraints, hobbies you have, or something else that works to gamify.

At this early stage, it's extremely important that you don't contaminate your ideas too much. You should refer to the gameplay experience you are striving for through the mechanics but avoid referring directly to other games. It's not because other games are bad for you in some way. Not at all. In fact, if you design games, you should make sure to play as many games as time allows.

The reason you shouldn't refer to other games when talking about mechanics is the subjectivity mentioned earlier. You risk mistaking dynamics from a game you like for the mechanics that are actually providing this dynamic. Not to mention that copying other games always risks becoming just a worse version of something better.

Once you have your own game up and running, you can definitely start comparing your game to other games and try to inform yourself from the best practices on display. But at that point, chances are that your game will start a life of its own and you don't have to use the crutch of reference-based design at all.

Ways to Derive Mechanics

- **A + B**: A fantasy action role-playing game with guns. (Fantasy Action Role-Playing Game + Shooting Mechanics.)

- **A – B**: A first-person shooter without gravity. (First-Person Shooter — Gravity.)

- **A in B**: A grand strategy game in an underwater city. (Grand Strategy in Underwater City.)

- **A but B**: A collectible card game but you play with a single hand of cards. (Collectible Card Game but Single Hand of Cards.)

- **A, extra B**: A racing game where the vehicles are much much faster. (Racing, Extra Speed.)

Ways to Invent Mechanics

- **Component interaction**: Flipping cards upside down, losing if you release a button, or jumping automatically. Use something recognizable differently.

- **Theme**: An interesting theme will often directly imply mechanics. Explore the different literary elements to see what comes out.

- **Activity**: Base-jumping, machine engineering, wood-cutting, math, or programming. Any activity can be a great inspiration for a mechanic.

- **Constraints**: If you can't do a thing, something has to replace it.

- **History**: An historical event that's strange, obscure, or simply very interesting.

- **Fiction**: A book, movie, or TV show that has a cool scene you want to turn into a game experience.

- **Hobby**: Cooking, stamp collecting, amateur theater, dancing, or weight-lifting. People have invented countless pastimes that could be excellent mechanics.

## DECIDE WHO THE PLAYER PLAYS

Deciding who your player is playing provides a way to look at your concept from more than one direction.

The player's avatar may be almost anything. A nation, an historical empire, a character, or a group of characters—games have tried many different types of avatars through the decades. The avatar may have a name, may be a very broad concept, or may be entirely abstract.

Picture a game about armed conflict, for example. There are countless ways you can build such a game. A few example avatars for players to control in an armed conflict (that still just scratches the surface) could be:

- You play a soldier following orders on the battlefield.
- You play an officer giving orders on the battlefield.
- You play part of an artillery crew firing a cannon.
- You play a high-ranking officer giving strategic orders.
- You play a correspondent, reporting on war crimes.
- You play a prisoner of war, trying to make it through.
- You play a U.N. chemical weapons inspector attempting to collect evidence.
- You play a politician telling the high-ranking officers what to do.
- You play the logistics of the military, shipping troops, food and ammunition to the front, and casualties away from it.
- You play the entire military.
- You play a whole nation.
- You play the political authority for the entire planet Earth.

### Defining an Avatar

1. Look at what the player will be doing in your game. If you have a list of verbs already, start from there.

2. Consider where this theme or these activities fit, and who would engage with them.

3. List all the "whos" you can come up with.

   a. **The facilitator**: Who is demanding or making the activities possible?

   b. **The doer**: Who is it that has to engage in all of the activities your facilitator has in mind?

   c. **The enemy**: Who opposes the activities you have in mind?

   d. **The instrument**: Someone stuck between the other three, minding their own business, yet somehow becoming embroiled anyway?

   e. One of these four could be your avatar!

4. Brainstorm other "whos" that may work, including things that may seem outlandish at first. It can be anything. An animal, a profession (plumber comes to mind), *etc.*

5. Go through the list of whos and consider each one and what it would mean:

   a. For the game's theme

   b. For the player(s)

   c. For the game's image, mood, and atmosphere

   d. For the game's marketing

6. Make a decision, even if that decision is to try two or more of the "whos" you've come up with to see which one sticks.

## ASSUME LESS

Whenever you say, "players want X," "players expect Y," or "it should work like in Z," instead find a way to evaluate it from the perspective of your own game.

Every time you skip doing something by letting an assumption get the better of you, you forget that the hugely successful *Fortnite* didn't exist before 2017, that deck builders became a prominent thing with *Dominion* in 2008, and that First-Person Shooters used to be played with the arrow keys and not mouse and keyboard or dual analog sticks. Even genre definitions like role-playing game (RPG) mean very different things to different generations of players.

Assume as little as possible—build your game, not someone else's.

It's fine to feel lost or search for easy ways out. This is normal. But make yourself aware that it's a problem and do your best to remind each other (or yourself) to check those assumptions.

Some projects will of course have built-in assumptions that you must simply bring into your conversations. If you work with an existing intellectual property, for example, or if you are making a sequel, some assumptions may be contractually obligated.

But even then, it's still good practice to check your assumptions and find ways to validate them.

Assumption Checks

- Do not resolve your ideas by referring to solutions in other games. You need to establish what your game should be doing first and what experience you want to give the player.

- Do not imply what players want or how players will feel. You can't know that yet. Instead, focus on what kind of experience you want to create and the shortest path to achieving it.

- Avoid jargon and abbreviations to the extent possible. Everyone won't agree with your definition of what ARPG or FPS means, and it's not a discussion you need to have yet—it will only waste time.

- Be wary of the word "must," particularly around features. No game must do a certain thing. This only leads to deadends and derivatives.

- Wait as long as possible before you bring standard gamer language into the conversation. Once you start speaking of things like "third-person camera" or "deckbuilding," you will also introduce subconscious assumptions on what those things mean and you will shrink your design space.

- Try not to assert peer pressure. When you say something like, "we did that once on a project, and it didn't work," you're not helping. This is even less valuable if no one was there with you and is therefore able to argue the lessons learned. If the lessons can be made use of in ideation, share them. But chances are that it's anecdotal or even incidental to the ideas being presented.

### ASSUME LESS

## START FROM CONFLICT

Conflict is central to western storytelling. Screenwriter Aaron Sorkin sums it up as intention and obstacle: "Somebody wants something. Something standing in their way of getting it."

This is a great way to get started, particularly with games having a long history of battles, combats, and fights already. Pure conflict is subject matter that everyone will recognize.

To set up a conflict, first define something worth fighting for. It can be a magical fantasy MacGuffin, military secrets, access to a remote location, the most heart-throbbing prom date, or enough food to survive the night. People have fought and killed, both literally and metaphorically, over the weirdest things through history, and in fiction it's rarely important what it actually is. A golden ring that turns you invisible is worth a few armies of death and destruction, if you say it is.

All most players will need to get onboard is the knowledge that what they're fighting for is better than what they're fighting against.

Next you set up the factions. The one with the intent and the one that's the obstacle. The other person or people that also want your prom date. The enemy army that is invading your home. The counterspy trying to stop you from stealing national secrets.

### Person against Person

A formidable foe. An agent of the enemy. The immediately obvious villain, or the secret traitor that you don't know about as the game begins.

### Person against Self

"I'm my own worst enemy," we sometimes say. When dealing with depression, anxiety, or just trying to break your own speed record, you are in conflict against self.

### Person against Nature

Whether chasing the hated white whale or trying to survive off the land with nothing but what you can scrape together, you are fighting against nature.

### Person against Society

Oppression, censorship, persecution, and all the other nasty things that society has done, does, and probably will continue doing, are conflicts of person against society.

Person against Technology

The breakthrough invention that changed society and the conflict it causes. Not necessarily as anti-technological luddism, but as a reflection on our humanity.

Person against the Supernatural

God, gods, magic, demons, spirits, spells, *etc*. But also faith, fate, destiny, good against evil, and other spiritual conflicts.

**PERSON V. PERSON**     **PERSON V. SELF**

**PERSON V. NATURE**     **PERSON V. SOCIETY**

**PERSON V. TECHNOLOGY**

**PERSON V. THE SUPERNATURAL**

## PRETEND TO PLAY

Sit down with a UI artist, tester, good friend, or someone else, and just pretend to play the game on a piece of paper or a whiteboard. Ask the toughest questions you can think of as you go along and answer them spontaneously. Keep a record of any questions you can't answer, so you can put some effort into them later.

If there's a character, draw a stick figure or find a good image to use. Give it a name if it doesn't have one or book a meeting to decide on a name later. The same thing if you run into an enemy or something else: just acknowledge that it's needed and move on.

Draw your way through a play session, mock up anything you realize you need, and push for quick natural answers to the questions that keep coming up. You're not defining anything at this point. This whole exercise is here to get you better acquainted with your game design, and it's vitally important that you don't get stuck on any specific detail.

Keep going and don't get bogged down talking about a single thing. Keep the rhythm and flow as close to the intended play sessions as possible. Take ample notes.

For a big or complex game, you may have to do this multiple times. For such a game, consider each of the steps in the "Running a Pretend Session" and whether you should do each of them as a separate pretend session. Once for the menus, once for character creation, and once for world exploration; every big game has its own requirements.

### Running a Pretend Session

1. **The first thing the player encounters**: The introductory cinematic, unboxing the game components, or whatever else may apply. How does it look, what is included, and what happens before play even starts?

2. **The process of starting your game**: Board setup, menu interactions, game modes available, whether any choices are made by you or for you.

3. **The typical in-game starting process**: Any onboarding or tutorial instructions and how they are presented. Quick start rules, optional customization, and difficulty settings—anything that applies.

4. **The game loop or game turn**: This is the real "game" in your game. Pretending to play a fight, a level, or a full round of game turns. You should probably repeat this process and change some of the parameters you have introduced, so that you get as much information

from the pretend session as possible. Different enemies, different game modes, and variable difficulties—whatever may apply.

5. **The process of quitting the game**: Anything a player has to do to end the game, no matter if it's just pressing the Escape key and answering "Yes" to a prompt that comes up or putting all components back in their box.

6. **Coming back to the game after quitting**: This normally starts from #1, but there can also be ways to make the transition from outside the game to back in the game faster. Think of them in your pretend session. Maybe a "Continue" option from the main menu, or a section in your game box that allows you to save the board state.

## HOLD STRUCTURED MEETINGS

Few things can waste time quite like meetings. Even when you're two people discussing a rule system for a role-playing game, discussions can veer off and cost both time and sanity.

Since many game designers—regardless of their level—are extremely passionate about the tiniest details of what they do, they can waste everyone's time in ways that only passionate creatives are capable of. This is not to say that other developers aren't as passionate. But we're talking about ideation here—the free for all chaos that many game designers thrive on and would want to go on forever. Therein lies the time sink.

A general rule is to have fewer and more specific meetings with clearly stated goals, plans of action, and prewritten agendas that are effectively moderated. This may sound tedious and bureaucratic, and if you're a single designer and not a team it doesn't apply to you, but it applies more often than you may think.

There's one of those clever memorable acronyms you can use to make sure that meeting goals are made relevant, and it's SMART:

- **S**pecific, so that everyone understands what the goal is about.

- **M**easurable, making sure that we will know if it succeeds or not.

- **A**chievable, since it's otherwise unnecessary to have an action plan for.

- **R**elevant, preferably for more than just the game designers.

- **T**imed, with a clear deadline and predetermined review process, so that it doesn't just fade into the background or goes on forever.

### Before the Meeting

1. Write an explicit goal for the meeting. Something you need to decide on, a task you need to assign, whether the thing should be removed or kept, *etc.* Something that's actionable and concrete.

2. Summarize the subjects related to the agenda, point by point.

3. Leave room for a final point simply called "Questions." During the meeting, push any questions that come up to this point. Make it your catch-all for things that would otherwise delay decision-making.

4. Before the meeting starts, let everyone know the agenda so they can prepare.

At the Meeting

1. Assign a moderator to keep things on topic.

2. Assign someone to take notes.

3. Moderate with a vengeance. Does it fit into this subject? By all means, continue. Does it not, but it fits into another one? Tell the person to make a note but postpone the conversation. Or move on to the relevant subject naturally, announcing to everyone that you're now moving on to point Y from point X. Make sure that the conversation stays on course.

4. At the end of the meeting, revisit the meeting goal. Make the decision and formulate the action plan (remember SMART). Write it down, along with all relevant notes as to why it was made the way it was made and assign someone to be responsible for execution and for the review process.

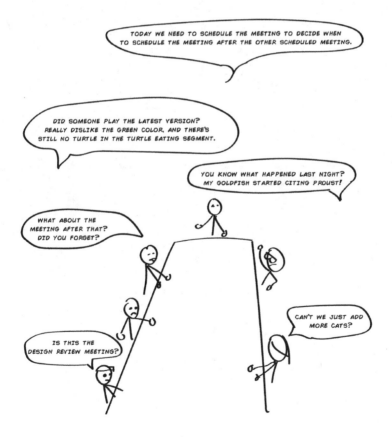

# CHAPTER 3

# Exploration

THERE ARE COUNTLESS WAYS to explore the results of your team's ideation. They are prototyping, setting up data in excel sheets, using pencils and paper, or printing tiny versions of all your cards on a single piece of paper just to be able to go through them all. There are many tools for exploration, and this stage in the design is where you make use of them.

Sometimes, you'll go back to ideation after exploration so you can iterate on the raw material that comes out. At other times, you'll decide that exploration has been successful or unsuccessful based on how it looks and feels, and you'll move on to Commitment.

This process is what may turn you into a Level 2 game designer, down the line, by making you more informed about your design.

What needs to come out of exploration is:

- Validation of which ideas work, and which need more work.

- Materials for more ideation, if you have the time to go back and forth.

- Records of what you learned from exploration, so that the lessons are not lost through time.

- Decisions on which ideas can simply be scrapped because they don't work as intended and which ones are worth keeping.

DOI: 10.1201/9781003332756-4

## SPOT THE SAUSAGE CAKE

Sausages are great and cake is great, so sausage cake has to be even greater! But whipped cream and chorizo don't mix very well, and the same is true in game design.

If you're mixing A and B together, what you risk doing is baking a sausage cake. Many brilliant games are hybrids of established genres, but you must learn to see when something is a functional hybrid design and when it's sausage cake.

One reason we end up baking these cakes can be compromise. If we don't have a vision holder—someone responsible for the overall concept of our game—there's a chance that we start accepting each other's ideas as a kind of tit for tat thing. I approve yours; you approve mine.

It can also be because we have very different disciplines and what engages us on a creative level varies. If one person really wants to design a game board, then we need to have a game board.

There's nothing inherently wrong with sausage cake in ideation, but exploration is where it should be caught, and it has to be decided whether it's a main course or a dessert.

### Spotting a Sausage Cake

- **Feature redundancy**: Having both guns and deadly spells kill enemies in similar ways and at a similar pace. This type of sausage cake may have aesthetic value but is rarely worth it for the gameplay experience. If you have multiple features available at the same time that yield the same result, at least one of them is probably unnecessary.

- **Feature creep**: This thing on the game board is a bit unclear, let's add a separate deck for it instead! Adding features to solve very specific problems, or for other spurious reasons, is often unnecessary. No, it doesn't need the sausage.

- **Stakeholder pleasers**: The producer likes guns, and the investor enjoys shoe shopping, so our third-person platformer will now support shooting and footwear customization. Features implemented to please stakeholders, rather than to make the game a better game. Sometimes you must do this to deliver your game, but in the best of worlds you have the authority to say no. Just remember that everyone is a Level 1 game designer—including stakeholders.

- **Following trends**: Played this cool game yesterday where there was this really cool set piece in a jungle, so let's add a jungle to our game! Doing things because another game does it, and not because it helps your project, will rarely improve your game's design.

- **Vanity features**: Features for the sake of one developer. This will be fun when it's done, I promise! This type of feature is a very common cause for sausage cakes. We let them stay to cut our colleagues some slack, but they don't always serve the game.

### DON'T BAKE SAUSAGE CAKE!

### IT'S DISGUSTING.

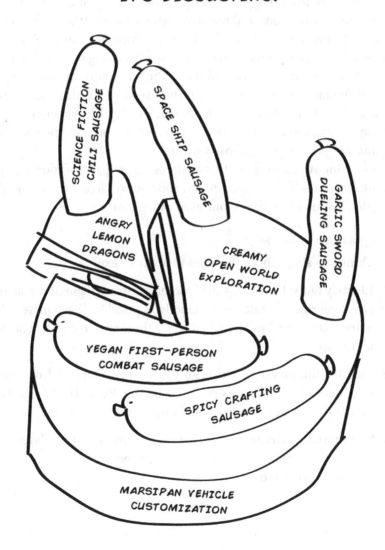

## MAKE ANALOG PROTOTYPES

Brenda Romero and Ian Schreiber wrote in their book, *Challenges for Game Designers*: "A painter gets better by making lots of paintings; sculptors hone their craft by making sculptures; and game designers improve their skills by designing lots of games."

With the turn-around time for even the simplest digital prototype counted in weeks and many games taking months or even years to prototype properly, analog game design can be a faster way to explore ideas.

Of course, if your whole idea is an analog game, this isn't just a tool; it's your whole process. For many digital game designers, it may even seem unintuitive.

But the same psychology applies to analog and digital games. Intrinsic and extrinsic motivations, and various motivational models, can be applied the same to every type of game. The same affordances apply. A playing card in a digital game is the same as that in an analog game, for example.

Analog games are systems laid bare. They are ideal for testing many types of digital mechanics in an informative way. It's also much easier to use a human player to represent complex things like enemy decision-making or procedurally generated systems before you start the process of defining and programming those systems.

By building an analog game that explores part or parts of your idea, you will inform yourself about your design and you will figure out things that work, don't work, or maybe no one even thought of.

Making a (Quick) Game

1. Think of a single thing you want to verify or explore.

2. **Identify facts**: List things that you have already figured out as true about your game, stated as succinctly as possible. "Each player plays a single character," is a potential fact. "There are ten different horses" is another.

3. **Identify the player(s)**: Artificial intelligence, simulated opponent, book-keeper, referee, or maybe game master. Each player can act as a simulator for a key system or take a direct part as a player.

4. **Summarize activities**: Now that you know who the players are, you sum up what they will be doing in the prototype and what it represents. The verbs.

5. **Gather components**: Once you know what the players will be doing, you have to figure out how to represent it with components.

   a. **Dice**: Roll, Reroll, Explode (roll again), Hide, Add/Subtract, Roll Equal or Below (<X), Roll Equal or Above (X+), and Custom Symbols.

   b. **Random tables, flowcharts, or sheets**, to represent generators, state machines, and player choices.

   c. **Cards**: Shuffle, Flip, Turn, Stack, Hide, Write Text, Pull, Steal, Draw, Discard, and Place in Grids or Tableaus.

   d. **Boards or terrain**: Can be just an empty table space, a grid, a custom-made board that represents the game's decisions, or something more elaborate.

   e. **Pawns or miniatures**: If you already have some 3D sculpts or other art, you should use it! Introducing some personality into an analog prototype makes a much bigger difference than anyone cares to admit.

### ANALOGUE LEVEL DESIGN!

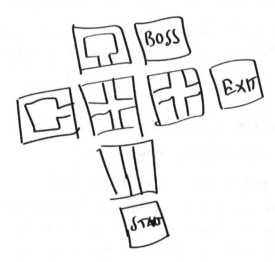

### WITH JUST PAPER, SCISSORS, AND A PEN, YOU CAN TEST MANY DESIGNS MUCH FASTER.

## USE TIMEBOXES

Timeboxing means setting a hard deadline, pre-planning what decision to make once you reach it, and then getting to work on proving the point you wanted to make.

If you have a new gun or a new feature you want to try out, timeboxing its validity to an hour, a day, a week, or some other timeline, means you are forced to cut corners to reach some representation of the end goal.

When time runs out, you can then test the feature and see if it's worth pursuing, or decide that it's not worth the effort.

This is a great way to let developers play with their ideas without affecting a wider schedule. It's also perfect for deciding what to commit to before really committing.

Where timeboxes truly shine is with spontaneous ideas. It's much too easy to just say no when someone comes up with an interesting idea. A timebox means you can say, "see what you can do in half a day," and then evaluate the idea on its real merits after that time has passed. The risk you must be aware of is that the timebox is set too small, which will set it up to fail and may cause some frustration.

For more casual projects, where time isn't as tightly tied to money, timeboxing is still highly useful, since it's way too easy to get stuck on just a small part of your game when there are many things to wrap up before you move on.

If you have a hard game design problem to solve, set up a timebox and once you hit it, the solution either gets cut or can be verified as a viable way forward.

Timeboxing

1. Set a goal, like a statement. "An enemy that runs much faster."

2. Set a hard deadline. "Tomorrow at lunch."

3. Assign a person who is responsible. "Programmer A."

4. Decide what to do if the timebox isn't successful. "Skip the idea of faster enemies." Remember to write this down as a decision, fact, or in some other way so that you don't bounce back in the future because you forget about it.

5. Decide what to do if the timebox is successful. "Schedule the fast enemy into a proper sprint."

The Size of a Timebox Must…

- Be shorter than a week, preferably shorter than a day.

- Fit within the chosen individual's current schedule and responsibilities without causing additional overtime.

- Leave no room for ambiguity. It must be a concrete deadline.

## TIMEBOXING

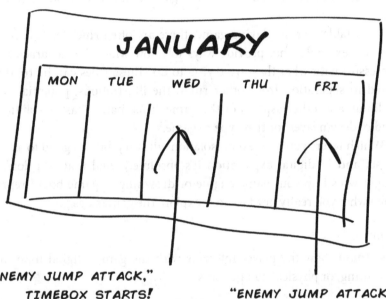

"ENEMY JUMP ATTACK,"
TIMEBOX STARTS!

"ENEMY JUMP ATTACK,"
TIMEBOX ENDS.
LEAD EVALUATES.

## DESIGN IN LAYERS

Exploration requires rapid iteration. You have to be able to isolate which parts you are working on, so you don't get overwhelmed. Maybe play without the cards for a few sessions, and then put them back in. Tweak something here, change something there. See what happens with different parts of the game when they have to work in isolation.

If this process is constantly sidelined by practical issues, such as a level crashing or the game board having to be reprinted, it costs valuable time that should be used for more exploration.

One solution is to consciously separate the design into distinct layers. A "layer," in this case, is a part of your game that isn't dependent on other parts.

For a tabletop role-playing game, there are often rules for task resolution, for example, that provide ways to know when their characters are successful with what they are trying to do. These rules can be tried and tested in separation from other rules, the illustrations, potential world building, and other aspects of the game. This makes "task resolution" a kind of design layer for that type of game.

Which layers you can test in isolation will vary, but it's good to actively do so, and in digital exploration it's absolutely vital that you don't get caught wrestling your game engine or drowning in game board reprints when what you really need to do is explore the game's design.

Example Layers

- **Input**: how the player interacts with the game. Digital input handling, or physical components.

- **Data**: number of cards, health, hand size, move speed, save files, optional settings, *etc*. Everything that needs to be specified can be tweaked separately from everything else.

- **Spawning**: how things are brought into and out of the game, including enemy spawns, cards, objectives, and much more. Level loading, procedural generation, and countless other techniques can be tweaked on this layer.

- **Smoothing**: how it feels to play, and how transitions are handled. Easing, frame blending, and phase separation are versions of smoothing.

- **Visuals**: how all the other things are represented, including visual fx, sound, music, models, illustrations, and so on.

- **Regions**: how you block off the game, physically or conceptually. Can be a level or part of a level in a 3D game, or a game board or specific area of a game board for a board game.

HMM... I WANT TO TRY THIS NEW WAY OF SPAWNING ENEMIES...

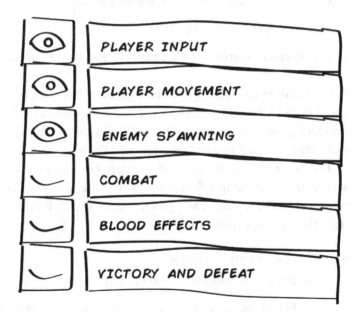

PLAYER INPUT

PLAYER MOVEMENT

ENEMY SPAWNING

COMBAT

BLOOD EFFECTS

VICTORY AND DEFEAT

IT HELPS TO LOOK AT YOUR GAME IN "LAYERS," AND TO MAKE SURE YOU CAN EXPLORE THOSE LAYERS IN ISOLATION!

## MAKE FLOWCHART PROTOTYPES

This is a mostly abstract form of prototyping, where you see how things fit together and use systemic inputs and outputs to see how well the idea works on a theoretical level.

First you should identify what's moving through the flowchart and what resources you are moving through the nodes. It can be handy to use physical components like cards and wooden cubes at this stage in prototyping, but it's of course not required.

Each node in the flowchart should have some kind of function, and some functional types are very handy here:

- A **source** generates a resource.

- A **stock** stores a resource.

- A **converter** turns one resource into another.

- A **sink** spends an amount of a resource.

- A **decider** determines what happens based on its access to resources.

If you think of the typical level up system, it has sources adding experience points (XP) to a stock. Once this stock contains a set amount of XP, a decider figures this out and sends the XP to a converter. This converter will then send spent XP to a sink and increase the level stock by one.

These five nodes can be used to represent almost any type of game system in a very simple flowchart. Any game idea with an exchange of resources—health, gold, cash, pawns, move speed, fuel, *etc.*—can benefit from this type of exploration.

Making a Flowchart Prototype

1. Decide which resources the flowchart will be using.

    a. **Finite resources** will run out and, once they run out, there's no more of them. Like your deck of cards, or *StarCraft* minerals.

    b. **Ascending resources** are better the more you get, like XP or cash.

    c. **Descending resources** have a cap and then descend as they are spent. Like health or stamina.

d. **Feature resources** are things you can spend to generate an interaction. A key, a grenade, or a Get Out of Jail Free card in *Monopoly*.

e. **Timed resources** run on timers or cooldowns and are made temporarily inaccessible by use but will then cycle back.

f. **Meta resources** are things external to the game. How much time the player has, how much table space there is, *etc*.

2. Identify the starting state of the resources and what kinds of outcomes are possible. Also consider whether there are choices to make at these points:

a. Resource runs out completely.

b. Not enough of the resource.

c. Just enough of the resource.

d. Too much of the resource.

e. Resource cap.

3. Use the five node types to draw a flowchart for the flow of resources, Source, Stock, Converter, Sink, and Decider.

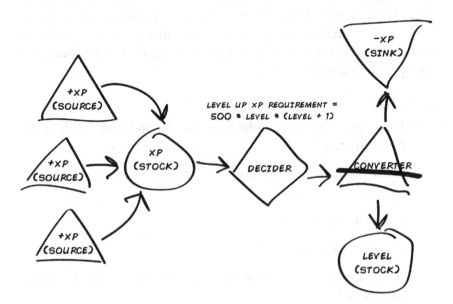

## ROLE PLAY YOUR DESIGN

If your game has characters or factions of any kind, role-playing them and/ or the world the avatar lives in makes it possible to explore morality, ethics, motivation, factional agendas, and a long range of other things about your game world.

Tabletop role-playing games can be seen as a kind of **formalized conversations**. You say what you do and you generate outcomes that steer the conversation in different directions. Sometimes you generate additional output using random chance or other gameplay mechanics, but this isn't strictly necessary. It's improvised make believe with game rules added for additional context. The game rules can be used to simulate the creation of the world or individual actions in the world.

To use this as a game design tool requires a process for **character creation**, if only to represent the potential avatars or factions, and their motivations. It also requires **rules**, either to determine what you can or can't do, or to add the potential for explicit representations of your game's features, such as guns, gear, experience points, buildings, and distances; whatever your game may need.

An added bonus of doing this work is that you'll have a ready character generator for fleshing out your world with more individuals later on, if you need them.

Character creation can start from the 5W+H interview technique: Who, What, Where, Why, When, and How. (We will revisit this again later, in the context of telling stories.) The intent is to cover the whole extent of a story, whether as a journalist writing a story or police officer interrogating a suspect.

Characters

1. **Who** the characters are, who they work for and with, and how they fit into the world.

2. **What** the characters do. List the activities you want them to take part in.

3. **Where** it takes place.

4. **Why** the characters do what they do.

5. **When** it takes place, whether past, present, future, or some specific time period.

6. **How**, for a game, means the verbs: your players' inputs and intentions.

Rules

1. **Situations**: what kinds of situations you want your game to portray. Are they heists, fights, competitions, planning projects, survival, *etc*?

2. **Abilities**: this sets the stage for who you are role-playing:

   a. What can they do, and what can't they do?

   b. What is particularly hard for them to do, but still possible, and what is especially easy for them but still relevant?

3. **Conflict**: keeping the situations and abilities in mind, who is trying to stop you, why, and by what means. Write rules for the conflicts that are most important—don't simulate, only represent.

4. **Stage**: where you are right now and what you are doing. Pick options from the Where and What you wrote about characters, and then go.

Play

1. Describe what your character does, staying true to that character.

2. If you are asked to speak, speak as your character would speak.

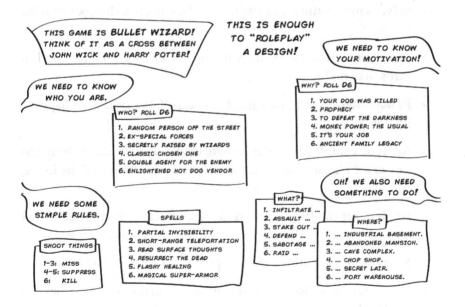

## ADD UNCERTAINTY

Game designer Greg Costikyan argues in the introduction to his book, *Uncertainty in Games*, that "games require uncertainty to hold our interest," and he then identifies several different types of uncertainty and how they relate to the design of different types of games.

When you start exploring your ideas, thinking about which types of uncertainty you want to include is a great way to remind yourself about the player's perspective. If you want the player to have an amazing story experience, it's all about Narrative Anticipation, and you must consider how to achieve this through your design.

Similarly, a competitive game may need enough Performance Uncertainty to require practice and allow for strategies and interactions, while also adding Player Unpredictability on top of that.

If you find that your game is too predictable or doesn't hold people's interest for long enough, you may consider the types of uncertainty and if you could add more of them.

Types of Uncertainty

- **Performance uncertainty**: can I make the jump, or finish the match?

- **Solver's uncertainty**: can I figure out how to open the door or solve the puzzle?

- **Player unpredictability**: does my opponent have a better hand of cards than me?

- **Randomness**: will I make the d20 check of 15+, and what happens if I don't?

- **Analytic complexity**: if the As hate the Bs, and my Cs are trying to spread the plague, and the Ds are currently revolting, and the Es, Fs, and so on.

- **Hidden information**: are there zombies down in the basement, and if so, how many, and is the loot down there worth the danger?

- **Narrative anticipation**: what happens when we open Pandora's Box?

- **Development anticipation**: this game is starting to look amazing, can't wait to put my hands on it!

- **Schedule uncertainty**: will I be able to play again, once my lives have replenished, or should I buy some more now?

- **Perception uncertainty**: can I parse the information correctly, and not get hit by one of the 10,000 projectiles streaming across the screen?

## MAGIC IT!

In the collectible card game *Magic: The Gathering*, you never see a card that's just a "bear:" it'll be a "Dragon-Scarred Bear," or a "Razorclaw Bear," or some other mix that sounds more menacing and inspiring, or conjures images of the world the game takes place in.

It takes the subject ("bear") and then adds relevant adjectives ("dragon-scarred") designed to reinforce what the card is about and to solidify where it fits into the world of the game. The difference is mostly a cosmetic one, but it allows the thing to be more memorable and much more atmospheric simply by careful selection of words.

Whenever you name something, whether it's a design pillar, section headline, in-game item, or other player-facing expression in your game, you can make great use of this same technique. You can **Magic It!**

To facilitate this, identify a number of adjectives, as custom and as relevant as possible, and put them in a list. Then write the things you need to convey using single words. It is even better if you set up specific rules for when to use certain adjectives. For example, one can be tied to a faction in the narrative, or to the interactions of a specific player.

Finally, go through the things you want to convey and append some of those adjectives to find out what makes the things more striking.

Make sure to never just call something a "bear" ever again.

Magicking Something

1. **Bring out the nouns** or other player-facing text that needs to be spiced up. It can also be developer-facing, for example the names of your design pillars, but it's most relevant for the things that will be player-facing down the line.

2. **Collect a list of adjectives**, potentially categorized based on what they are intended to communicate. It helps to write rules for these categories. For example, "use a synonym for darkness when describing an evil faerie."

3. In creating your adjectives, don't be afraid to append words the way many European languages do. Remove hyphens. "Nightborn" or "Blacknight" can make for something more striking and unique than night-born or black-night. But keeping the hyphen can also be done to emulate certain styles of writing.

4. **Append the Adjectives**. Do multiple takes of the same thing, with the same objects. "Nightborn Faerie." "Blacknight Faerie." For a game pillar, calling something "Fast-Paced Combat" says nothing, but "Two-Second Kills" does!

## THINK OF THE DATA

While exploring, it's sometimes helpful to remind yourself to not think like a user. No matter how unintuitive this feels to the modern user experience-aware game designer.

The goal of this tool is to help maximize the number of iterations you have time to do during exploration, and it has two specific components that are both from software development in general: making things object-oriented and data-driven.

Object-oriented can be thought to mean that things are defined by their isolated behavior. An object describes a single logical piece of your game. Think of characters, for example. In your game, maybe characters move and shoot. **Character** is an object and contains things like the name of the actual character and maybe what team it belongs to. **Mover** could be another object and all it does is move whoever makes use of it. **Gun** is another object and keeps track of all the gun-related shenanigans in your game. As an example, an enemy soldier **IS** a character, and it **HAS** a rifle and also **HAS** a mover.

That is all well and good—we can now define the behavior of our game entities by **has-a** and **is-a** relationships. But they also need data.

The instinct is often to write a number straight into your code, and then go back and forth between simulation and implementation. But the best thing you can do is to decouple the numbers from the logic to as large an extent as possible. Make the logical objects operate as they do, and then plug the data into them as external resources.

This is true for analog games as well, for example by having cards refer to external variables rather than crisp data.

### Object-Oriented

**Is-a:** enemy **is-a** character, bicycle **is-a** mover, and card **is-a** gun. What type of object we're talking about, and all its connected behavior.

**Has-a:** enemy **has-a** gun, bicycle **has-a** rider, and card **has-a** stats bar. What type of component we're talking about, and how it therefore affects the owning object.

### Data-Driven

**Baseline:** A baseline number is plugged in everywhere it's relevant and may then be tweaked globally to alter how the game behaves. An example is a damage baseline that all enemies use, which can be set higher for harder difficulties. Another example is the level in an experience economy that can be plugged into anything—movement speed, jump height, sight range, global card count, and so on.

**Attributes**: Object-specific attributes, like movement speed, melee damage, match time, card hand size, *etc*. Remember that objects aren't just game world entities. Game modes, objectives, game board spaces, clickable menu buttons, and so on are also objects.

**Modifiers**: World or context modifiers. Things like the decrease in friction when you're moving on ice, the +1 you should add to damage and to hit chances from your magical longsword, or a card on the table that says everyone draws an extra card each turn. Any data that **modifies** an attribute or baseline number is a modifier.

**Functions**: Think in terms of baseline, attributes, and modifiers; then smash them together. Whether you're adding, dividing, multiplying, or employing complex trigonometry is up to your design.

| BASELINE | ATTRIBUTES | MODIFIERS | FUNCTIONS |
|----------|-----------|-----------|-----------|
| ATTACK DAMAGE | STRENGTH ATTRIBUTE (BONUS DAMAGE) | SENSITIVITY TO FIRE (BONUS DAMAGE) | BASELINE + STRENGTH + FIRE - ARMOR = TOTAL DAMAGE |
| JUMP HEIGHT | PLAYER JUMP HEIGHT | SUPERJUMP BOOTS | JUMP HEIGHT + PLAYER JUMP HEIGHT + (SUPERJUMP BOOTS) = TOTAL JUMP HEIGHT |
| MAX CARD COUNT | PLAYER HAND SIZE | EXTRA CARD DRAW ABILITY | TURNS PER GAME = MAX CARD COUNT / CARD DRAW PER TURN |

IF YOU CAN GO IN AND TWEAK NUMBERS INDIVIDUALLY-- BASELINE, ATTRIBUTES, MODIFIERS-- THIS MAKES IT A LOT EASIER TO EXPLORE YOUR DESIGN!

## ADD ROUGH EDGES

Imagine playing a game about going from one place to another, and nothing happens along the way. You set off on your journey, walk some and run some, and suddenly you're at your goal and you watch the end credits.

It can sometimes happen while you're exploring your game that you simply find it a bit bland, just like a fictional journey without a hitch. When you do, there are some rough edges you can add to the currently polished experience. A rough edge in this context is **any kind of cost**.

The most common cost is time, since having to redo things or retread paths is universally annoying and works almost no matter what game you are making. From forcing you to skip a turn in a board game (something you should never do) to having you return to your dead body as a ghost after a fatal altercation with an angry goblin.

Time costs can be replaced by other costs. Any resource works: from gold to stamina to extra lives or discarding cards. What's important is that the cost makes intuitive sense and becomes something the player can plan for and handle in interesting ways.

### Adding Rough Edges

- **Don't explain**: some game features may become more powerful if you don't talk about them but let the player find them instead. Puzzle solutions usually belong here, but also synergies that appear organically from your features; what designers like to call **emergent** features.

- **Add challenge**: make the things the player does often hard to do. The trail is slippery or full of cacti, an angry troll guards the door, or nightfall makes everything dark.

- **Lock the door**: make the most obvious way forward inaccessible, so that the player is forced to find another way or break through.

- **Take things away**: once the player gets too comfortable with a feature or option, remove it or make it ineffective. Maybe the regular jump is no longer high enough, or the four-sided die can't roll the six or higher that's needed.

- **Add traps**: traps can be obvious, like giant pits with spikes at the bottom, or they can be more devious, like choosing the health potion from three different red flasks. Once players become aware that there can be traps, they will be more cautious.

- **Add treasure**: you can also sprinkle rewards instead of traps. They can be collectables, boosts in some resource, pieces of lore, or just fun things to feel clever about finding. Whatever they are, it adds a time cost to search for them.

- **Look, don't touch**: show cool things that you don't let the player interact with. Behind bars, far away on a map, or restricted by game progression.

- **Touch, don't taste**: let the player interact with things, but limit their usefulness. A cool gun without ammo. An upgrade slot, but no upgrade to put there.

ADD ROUGH EDGES!
MAKE IT COST SOMETHING TO
GO FROM 'HERE' TO 'THERE'.

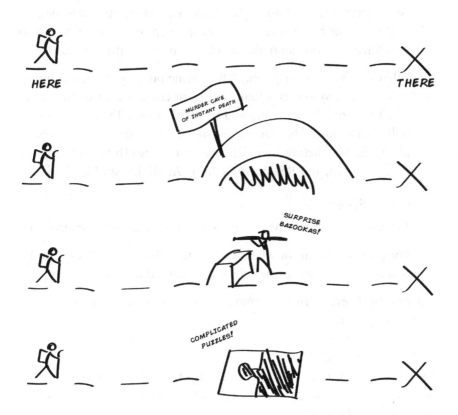

## INPUT, OUTPUT, SCREAM

Deep in the underpinnings of your game, you have what Michael Sellers calls the "spreadsheet specific" information in his book, *Advanced Game Design: A Systems Approach*. Health 100. Damage 15.

But you may also have a health system that deals with things like regeneration, different damage types, armor absorbing some incoming damage, and so on. This health system is now part of a network of inputs and outputs, with resources and data shared between them. Now just add player feedback and your system is ready to join all the other systems that make interesting gaming happen.

**Inputs** are things that you plug into the system in question. Health 100 could be the baseline health input, but any data, resource, or even player interaction that the health needs to know about is an input of some kind.

**Outputs** are then what's generated by the result of all that input. When some damage is sent into the health system, what pops out is the current health or maybe the current health percentage as an output so that other systems can make use of it—say, the death system.

**Feedback** isn't always required, but at some point, you must communicate what a system is actually doing, or chances are that the player won't realize it's happening and think it's a bug. The health system will need to notify the player when they get hurt and at certain points along the way before they die. Maybe half health turns the green health bar red, and 10% makes it blink. All of that stuff is feedback.

Designing a System

1. **Inputs**: all the things the system needs. Resources, data, or anything.

2. **Outputs**: the result of whatever it is that the system does. Can be manipulated inputs, game behavior, or something else.

3. **Feedback**: events that communicate what the system is up to directly to the player.

Attract (A + A = Trigger)

When two things meet, they trigger an effect. In *Thief: The Dark Project* and other Dark Engine games, this style of behavior was referred to as Act/React, or Stim/Response.

When a burning torch touches something flammable (FireStim+FireResponse), for example, or when a water arrow hits a burning torch (WaterStim+WaterResponse), the responding object will have a predefined behavior (output) based on the stim in question (input), and maybe that means it's set on fire (feedback).

## Repulse (A − A = Trigger)

When two traits are disconnected, an effect happens. A weight is removed from a button. Behavior can be defined by which traits an object carries, the same as for attraction, but the trigger is reversed.

## Abstract (A <-> B <-> A)

Output and input don't interact directly, but with an abstract intermediary. The burning thing generates a flame, and the flame ignites the flammable thing. The flammable thing doesn't need to know about the torch that carries the flame.

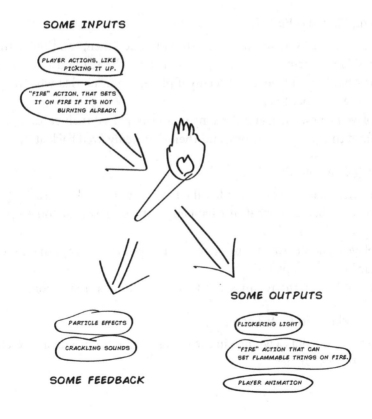

### A TORCH SYSTEM!

SOME INPUTS

PLAYER ACTIONS, LIKE PICKING IT UP.

"FIRE" ACTION, THAT SETS IT ON FIRE IF IT'S NOT BURNING ALREADY.

SOME OUTPUTS

PARTICLE EFFECTS

CRACKLING SOUNDS

FLICKERING LIGHT

"FIRE" ACTION THAT CAN SET FLAMMABLE THINGS ON FIRE.

PLAYER ANIMATION

SOME FEEDBACK

## CHALLENGE PLAY WITH PLOT

Everyone doesn't think of the game experience as a story and some games don't care too much about story to begin with. But if you listen to players who have played a game tell it, it often comes out as a kind of story anyway.

I did this, rolled the dice, and drew the card, then you did that, and these things happened, and now you're mad because someone has already bought the street you're on.

This is incredibly handy, because in the spaces between how a player tells this story you can find ways to continue exploring your game design. This may also tell you something about what players are finding interesting, which doesn't have to be the same things you find interesting.

When you analyze something this way, list how a player is describing their experience one event at a time. An event, in this case, is each individual interaction the player does plus each instance of game output this generates. String them together and you have a description of the "player story" that a particular player experienced. But you also have a chance to go in at each point where two events intersect—and put a twist there to see if you can make things more interesting.

### Turning Play into Plot: Then…

The most linear way to build forward is to add "then," and move things along. It may seem self-explanatory, but it can be really useful to think about what happens next. Especially if players indicate that what they are doing is a bit repetitive.

I played a new card, and **then** my opponent played their card.

I fired the gun many times, and **then** the enemy fired back at me.

### Turning Play into Plot: But…

Right after an event you have identified, you can insert the word "but" and use this to challenge what just happened. It forces you to come up with changes to the structure.

I played a new card, **but** my opponent played another card that canceled the card that I just played.

I fired the gun many times, **but** then I ran out of ammunition.

### Turning Play into Plot: Therefore…

Once the "but" puts a wrench in the works, you're ready with a "therefore" to take things further.

My opponent played another card that canceled my card; **therefore**, I was forced to end my turn.

My gun ran out of ammunition; **therefore**, I switched to the knife.

## BUILD TASK FORCES

One of the most common pitfalls when you explore part of a game—or a whole game idea—is that you end up wasting most of your time on other things. The simple answer of this tool is to not waste time.

If you're exploring a worker placement mechanic, don't waste time designing the visuals for the board. If you're making a combat system, don't waste time fighting the complex animation systems or getting the visual effects right—just get placeholder frames in there so that you can focus on the combat system and not on wrestling the game engine.

One practical way of doing this is to put together a cross-disciplinary **task force**. This group should include developers with valuable expertise both for having opinions and for making it happen. It's a task force and not a think tank.

This group is formed around a specific concept that needs to be tested, and the mixed nature of the expertise means that the delay between discussion and action will be as short as it can possibly get.

The main responsibility of the task force is to make sure that you stay focused on the singular goal you are working toward.

If you're a solo developer or a small team, you can mimic this by avoiding putting on any extra hats and to act as only the artist, or as only the game designer. It'll be a task force of one, of course, but many great games have been constructed this way.

### Setting Up a Task Force

1. Come up with the focus area of the Task Force. Shooting, scoring, assault rifle balancing, card description writing, or loot system; it can be anything, but must be specific.

2. Put a group together including everyone whose disciplines are affected by the focus area. For shooting, you probably need a programmer, a first-person animator, an FX artist, and maybe a creative owner—a Level 3 or 4 game designer. It's absolutely imperative that the group can work autonomously with what it comes up with and doesn't have to defer to external decision-making.

3. Schedule regular meetings with this Task Force—at least once a week—maybe even move the task force together physically at the office if you have an office.

4. At these meetings, set quick iterative goals. Use timeboxes for all goals and avoid discussing the things too much before you have results.

5. Evaluate things and set up new goals with new timeboxes at every meeting, constantly moving forward with only the specific task the task force started with.

DEPARTMENTALIZATION:
EVERY DISCIPLINE ISOLATED

TASK FORCE:
CROSS-DISCIPLINARY FOCUS

# CHAPTER 4

# Commitment

A T SOME POINT YOU need to commit to the things that work and abandon the things that don't. This is where you do that!

In the best of worlds, you can commit gradually through an iterative back-and-forth between ideation and exploration. But it may also become an abrupt cutoff where you have ramped up your hiring process and must switch to production before the money runs out.

Committing to a design is extremely hard and you'll be tempted to keep exploring and even ideating after committing. Don't.

Commitment in this case should be real. A hard divider between ideation/exploration and delivering a finished game.

What you need to commit to is:

- A working definition of your game that everyone has approved: designers, developers, stakeholders, and everyone.

- What the game is about.

- What to make; what not to make.

- Production and testing timelines.

- Priorities: Musts, Needs, Shoulds, and Wants.

DOI: 10.1201/9781003332756-5

## TELL A STORY

A big deal when it's time to commit is to explain your game to other people. To stakeholders, publishers, your team, and your kids; everyone, over and over again.

As you probably know, people's eyes glaze over when you start extrapolating on the neat details of your fabulous new core mechanics, since the jargon of game development is much denser and harder to interpret than we may want to admit.

But people are narratively biased and respond well to stories. Acknowledge this, and make sure to have good answers to all of the implied questions. Tell a story when you describe your game, and don't describe the game. Make the description incidental, almost accidental.

The immediately relatable will resonate better with an audience. Some people are never interested in what happens in Fantasyland but may care about the personal financial struggles of a Fantasyland character. A businessperson will want to know how much your game may sell and a writer may want to know your literary inspirations.

Then there's blood. Still preferable if it's relatable, so we can think we're glad it didn't happen to us, but violence and its effects can be fascinating in its own right. It also doesn't have to be literal blood. Other risks may be enough, like debt, damage, injury, and so on.

### Telling a Story

In interviews, interrogations, and other contexts where you want to get the full picture of what's happened, 5W+H is a kind of reminder, so you don't forget any of the pieces that tell a complete story.

1. **Who** is the player portraying, who is the game about, or whose perspective will the game focus on?

2. **What** will the player be doing, or what is the player's alter ego doing? Can be expressed as something about to happen, or something that's already happening. Leave the listener wondering and wanting more.

3. **Where** does the game take place? Whatever you do—don't go into lengthy explanations unless people ask you to.

4. **Why** is the player or alter ego supposed to be doing what they'll be doing? Think about motivations and goals, and remember to make sure they are worth rooting for.

5. **When** does it take place? Can be expressed as technology level, or as a time and place. Can be completely fictional, but may still use terms like "long ago," "once upon a time," or "in the distant future," to give a bit of context.

6. **How** are things supposed to work out? If there is a specific story to tell, explain a couple of major beats. Give the listener something to get excited about.

> IT'S A FAST-PACED TACTICAL DYNAMIC RPG/FPS/RTS.

> TAKES ITS INSPIRATION FROM BATTLEMURDER III, RELEASED IN ONLY 5 DELUXE COPIES IN EARLY 1984.

> IT'S THE NEAR FUTURE, AND MANKIND IS ON THE VERGE OF CLIMATE COLLAPSE.

> YOU CONTROL A SECRET ORGANIZATION TASKED WITH SOLVING THIS COLLAPSE.

> YOU WILL SOMETIMES HAVE TO SNEAK INTO ENEMY TERRITORY ALONE; AT OTHER TIMES, YOU WILL LEAD SMALL FORCES OF ELITE UNITS AGAINST THE EXTRATERRESTRIAL CONSPIRACY.

## BUILD AN AMUSEMENT PARK

Telling a story is one way to talk about your game. The other is to sell an experience and talk about your game as if it's not just a ride but a whole amusement park full of rides.

As you arrive at the park, you're treated to a massive area with endless options for dining, shopping, and entertainment. You unfold the map and begin the family battle of deciding where to go first, where to go next, and figuring out where the bathrooms are. You'll say yay or nay until a plan takes shape.

Maybe you go on the big rollercoaster, or you go to the wizard's shop to get shocked at the price of a plastic wand replica. No matter what you do, each thing is short and sweet and leaves you wanting more. Even if you ride the rollercoaster several times, the fear that you might die makes it worth it.

In your own time, at your own leisure, you've figured out what to do—done it—and moved on. The day eventually ends, and you go back to your hotel.

New rides are sometimes added, and old rides are removed. But the experience of going to an amusement park makes it worth doing over and over again without changing it too much. There's even a fair chance that removals would meet customer chagrin because they had all looked forward to doing that thing again that they did last time.

Now let's apply the same thinking to your game. Describe the game as an amusement park, starting with arrival, what options are available, and how the experience develops from there.

For some kinds of games, this is a lot more fitting than telling a story.

Building a Theme Park

1. **Arrival**: if it is a boxed game, digital download, or something else.

2. **Rides**: what you get to do in this game that you don't get to do in other games.

3. **Conveniences**: how the experience outside the main play activities works.

4. **Departure**: how quitting works, and what ways you make it easy to come back.

# 1) ARRIVAL
### (AND RETURN!)

# 2) RIDES
### (GAME LOOPS; MAIN ATTRACTIONS)

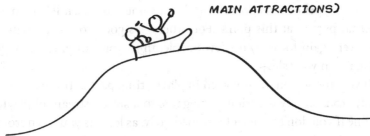

## 4) DEPARTURE

## 3) CONVENIENCES

## SAY IT AGAIN

Presentation—whether storytelling or design talk—requires confidence. No matter how well you think you know your project, there are almost always questions that will stop you dead in your tracks. Things you hadn't thought about or never considered important.

To gain that confidence, a great way to commit to your design is to present the same thing over and over and over again. You will get more comfortable and plug holes you'd otherwise miss every time you go through the motions. It gets even better if you have some pressure when you do the presentations. Maybe have a producer push you, or present to your team over and over. Asking the same questions, demanding faster answers. If you don't get at least a little frustrated, they aren't pushing you hard enough.

The game design needs to survive the scrutiny of all disciplines and all potential types of consumers as well. For some projects, it'll help to include external parties at this point. For others, it's good to just present it over and over again to the same few people, until you can practically present the game in your sleep.

If you are personally involved in playtesting, part of this will come naturally from simply describing the game to a steady stream of playtesters. It's fine if you don't get it right immediately, as long as you learn from your mistakes and improve your ability to read social cues.

Learning to spot when someone finds you boring is maybe the most fundamental skill you will ever need as a game designer.

### Retelling

- Present only the hook of your project and revise it each time you present it. How do you present the hook to an artist? To a programmer? To an investor? To another game designer? Try all of them, even if you only have your mirror as a stand-in.

- **Whatever you do**: never get defensive. If someone has questions, either answer them correctly or say that you don't know and note the question as a potential problem. Even if you know it's not important, you pretend that it is.

- **Another thing**: never make excuses. No one wants to hear them. It's better to just keep going than to make excuses when you are trying to build engagement.

- Have someone you can present to over and over that is also able to push you to answer questions and correct yourself until it's no longer needed.

- Practice! If you have a 10-minute pitch, present it again and again until you've done it for a whole workday. You gain confidence, and you figure out answers to questions people will be asking you anyway.

## DEFINE THE FEATURES

The player may be rolling dice, navigating a 3D world, saving/loading, shuffling the deck of cards, managing inventory, *etc*. Meanwhile, the player's avatar is shooting, jumping, running, questing, and maybe invading Rome.

Having already had all the ideas and explored them, you now need to write a list of the features your game will actually make use of. The list shouldn't be too long, but still needs to encompass both the obvious and the not so obvious ones. It doesn't have to be complete right away, but before you move on to the green pastures of Problem Solving, they have to be made as complete as can be.

Your design style and preferences will dictate how thorough you are with your feature list, but as a rule, you should always list the direct features of the avatar and player. It's not unusual for a list of this kind to have a couple of hundred entries, but it's relevant to avoid duplicates.

Just remember that this is a **player-facing** exercise. Avoid thinking too much about the developer tools and fancy things you have going on behind the scenes. This tool is all about the game a player will be playing—not how it gets made.

Some of the features that you should think of at this stage are things you don't want players to do that you know they will do anyway. In games with a social component or custom content opportunities, you should consider players' avenues for creating offensive content or harassing other players in different ways. Those are also "features," even if you'd prefer them not to be, and you will need to at least be aware of them as you move forward.

Obvious Features

- **Verbs**: Once more, the verbs! Attacking, Defending, Aiming, and Drawing Card. Jumping, Crouching, Dodging, Avoiding Detection, and Swimming.

- **Events**: Consequences of things that happen in the game, like success and failure. Dying, Winning, Losing, Quitting, Unboxing, and Packing Away.

- **Feedback**: Falling, Exploding, Stumbling, Discarding, and Restarting.

Less Obvious "Features"

- **Hardware verbs**: Unplugging the Network, Glitching, Losing Input, Lagging, Crashing, and Vibrating.

- **Player verbs**: Ignoring Instructions, Leaving Game Running, Forgetting to Save, and Misinterpreting.

- **Fault verbs**: Lost Components, Broken components, Corrupt Save Files, and Bad Performance.

- **Social verbs**: Cursing, Rage-Quitting, Slandering, Harassing, Befriending, Blocking, Muting, Swearing, and Offending.

### FEATURES

SHOOTING
JUMPING
DRAWING
DYING
FLYING
DISCARDING
WINNING
LOSING
MOVING

### ALSO FEATURES

EXPLODING
BURNING
QUITTING
SCORING
GUI MESSAGING
MINIMAP
CRAFTING
COLLECTING
DECK SHUFFLING
RAGE-QUITTING

A FEATURE IS PLAYER-FACING.

A THING THE PLAYER INTERACTS WITH OR THAT INTERACTS WITH THEM.

## STAND ON PILLARS

Many game designers talk about **design pillars**. The analogy is of course pillars that support a building's roof. Design pillars support a game design's roof as well. If designed well, the roof prevents the torrent of ideas from turning into a leaking trickle of doubt that ultimately collapses the building.

It sometimes helps to look at a design pillar as an Internet meme. A "meme" is thought of as a unit of cultural information transferable from one mind to another almost like the transfer of genes between generations of organisms. This is exactly what a game design pillar needs to do. Its job is to remind everyone of the project's principles.

A single line of text or an image and a single line, and all you need to do going forward is reinforce it through repeated and consistent use. Have a bit of fun with it, too, just like you do with memes. Fun can make the point come across more effectively.

When it works, it'll become a consistent descriptor for your project that can be used across disciplines to communicate what your game is about and repeated almost instinctively as an answer to tricky questions.

Just avoid making the pillar too generic. "Fast-paced combat" doesn't mean anything without context, for example. "Single-hit kills" or "Five-second fights" would say more.

### Building a Pillar

- **Transferable**: The pillar has to be easy to say and easy to "memeify." No more than a single sentence; preferably fewer than five words. If you can find a good image or play on a well-known Internet meme to get it across more efficiently—even better.

- **Broad**: Pillars need to be broad enough to include a large part of your game and should imply both gameplay and theme, if possible.

- **Overlapping**: Pillars should overlap different parts of your game and shouldn't be useful only for the game design. Consider what "five-second fights" means for the animators, or "one-card hand" means for the card artists.

- **Specific**: Pillars may have to be broad, but they also shouldn't be too broad. Each should apply to a specific part of the game and make it easier to talk about the game's creative goals. A pillar intended for gameplay, like "five-second fights," will of course imply how things will look visually as well; but it's mostly concerned with gameplay and its many connected disciplines.

- **Unique**: Each pillar has to be unique. There may sometimes be some thematic overlap, but having more than one pillar say similar things easily gets confusing. If you have combat, for example, only one pillar should touch on combat even if other pillars may imply things related to the combat.

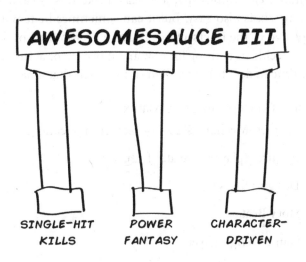

## CROSS-MATRIX EVERYTHING

This tool is particularly useful when you get stuck or can't think of good solutions to a particular problem.

A cross-matrix is a grid table where you assign some concepts to the rows and some other concepts to the columns. Each intersection between column and row helps you identify an important synergy that you will need to address, or a specific game interaction that you need to figure out.

Finding two things that are related like this is easy. Putting it into a cross-matrix is also easy. But it can sometimes be tempting to skip over one or two of the intersections because it's too hard or feels too abstract. Don't. Decide something for now and move on, or at the very least set aside some time to decide it later. Remind yourself that it needs to be decided.

Example Concepts to Cross-Matrix

- Themes, Mechanics, or Conflicts from ideation

- Features (player or avatar features)

- Design Pillars

- Story Beats

- Game Design Layers

- World Factions

Making a Cross-Matrix

1. Draw a simple grid, preferably on a whiteboard, or open a new document in a spreadsheet program.

2. Assign some set of concepts to the rows, for example, Features.

3. Assign another set of concepts to the columns, for example, Design Pillars.

4. Using the grid, write a short description at each intersection that defines how that intersection behaves. At the intersection between the "Five-Second Fights" pillar, and the "Shooting" feature, you have to figure something out. Now you're doing game design!

## Combination Matrix

Picture a game where you use combinations of artifacts to achieve magical effects. If you have one artifact that lets you turn invisible and another that sets you on fire, you will need to decide whether one should cancel out the other or if it's fine that the fire turns invisible along with the character.

Then you add freezing, and levitation, and a bunch of other things, and suddenly you need to know how each of them combines with every other thing.

A combination checklist lets you do this in a simple form. You list all the artifacts in a cross-matrix, and each time you add a new one you add it as both a row and column. This forces you to decide how a new artifact combines with all other artifacts and makes sure that you don't forget any edge cases.

| | SINGLE-HIT KILLS | POWER FANTASY | CHARACTER-DRIVEN |
|---|---|---|---|
| SHOOTING | ONLY COVER SAVES ANYONE FROM A SINGLE-HIT KILL | ALL THE GUNS ARE SUPER-BIG AND FIRE EXPLODING STUFF! | EVERY CHARACTER HAS A UNIQUE GUN THAT REFLECTS THEIR PERSONALITY |
| JUMPING | MISSING A JUMP TELEPORTS YOU BACK TO ATTEMPT AGAIN | YOU JUMP SUPER HIGH, AND THE ENVIRONMENT LOOKS LIKE REAL STUFF SO YOU GET A SENSE OF SLIGHT VERTIGO. | EVERY CHARACTER HAS A SET OF UNIQUE JUMP ANIMATIONS AS WELL AS LANDING AND JUMPING EFFECTS. |
| DRAWING | IF YOU DRAW THE LAST CARD, YOU DIE. | ALL CARDS HAVE AN EXTREME EFFECT, BENEFICIAL OR DETRIMENTAL. | EACH CHARACTER ALSO HAS A DECK OF UNIQUE CARDS. |
| DYING | DYING IS QUICK, AND INSTANTLY RELOADS. | NO DEATH LOOKS CHEAP. ALWAYS LARGER THAN LIFE! | CHARACTERS HAVE UNIQUE DEATH ANIMATIONS. |
| FLYING | IF YOU FLY INTO OBSTACLES, YOU DIE. | YOU FLY REALLY REALLY FAST! | THE METHOD OF FLYING IS DIFFERENT FOR EACH CHARACTER. |

## FACTUALIZE

A 'fact' is a simple statement that defines an aspect of the game and has been established beyond any shadow of doubt by everyone involved in the game's decision-making.

Each fact should be just a few words, no more than a single sentence, that clearly defines the agreed-upon thing.

**Our hero is Milla the Caterpillar,** is a fact. **A player may carry any two guns,** is another. **The player uses WASD or the left analog stick to move,** is one of those facts you need to establish too—even if it may sound self-explanatory and may clutter your lists of facts unnecessarily. **This level takes 10 minutes to complete,** is another fact, and may be stated as a goal before the level is built or as an established fact after the fact.

Each fact should be short, concise, and approved by everyone working on whatever thing it applies to. Once established, you can refer back to the facts continuously throughout your work. Both as an approval process and as a reminder of the things you have already decided.

Unlike pillars that may be malleable through the course of a project, facts should stay as they are from the moment they're defined and until the project is delivered. Because of this, it's better to discuss things in loose terms before defining a fact so everyone is onboard with what is defined.

You don't have to use all of a game's established facts all the time, however, but can cherry-pick which ones you care most about at every stage. You can also choose to actively make exceptions if you want to provide the player with a specific experience in a certain part of the game. Just make sure everyone agrees first. It takes a deep understanding of established facts before you can make exceptions.

### Writing a Fact

1. Once a thing has been agreed upon in the team, figure out a way to state it as a fact, and then write a concise positive single-sentence statement. Positive means it should say "you may have three cards on hand" rather than "you may not have more than three cards." This may sound trivial, but it does make a difference in clarity.

2. Send the statement to everyone affected by it to get their approval. Even if they said they agreed initially, there may be nuances in phrasing that affects their opinion.

3. Collect all facts in an easily accessible place. A wiki, shared document, cloud service, or somewhere else that fits the project's requirements for security and accessibility.

## Using Facts

- For one-pagers, adding lists of related facts.

- When planning tasks for developers working on related systems or content, supply lists of relevant facts.

- As design reminders, point out the facts you have already agreed on, and take particular care when people want to make exceptions.

- To serve as a common ground for everyone working on the game, and as an accessible introduction to newcomers.

# *AWESOMESAUCE III FACTS!*

- ONLY COVER SAVES ANYONE FROM A SINGLE-HIT KILL.
- EVERY CHARACTER HAS A UNIQUE GUN THAT REFLECTS THEIR PERSONALITY.
- IF YOU DRAW THE LAST CARD, YOU DIE.
- IF YOU FLY INTO OBSTACLES, YOU DIE.

AT THIS POINT, YOU CAN COLLECT STATEMENTS ABOUT YOUR GAME THAT EVERYONE HAS AGREED ON.

THESE ARE **FACTS** ABOUT THE GAME AND ITS DESIGN.

## WRITE ONE-PAGERS

Communication is one of the most challenging aspects of a game designer's job. Though the traditional go-to is the giant bible-size tome often known as a Game Design Document (GDD), the truth is that few developers read those documents. GDDs are more likely to be required deliverables for a publisher's or other stakeholder's benefit.

You can absolutely keep a GDD for your own sake if you are the kind of designer who uses writing as part of your process. It can be used to keep track of all the ins and outs of your game, or to serve as a personal sounding board. With a board game or role-playing game design, this is likely to be the actual rules document. But to communicate design, you should definitely explore the wonders of the **one-pager** instead of the GDD.

A one-pager is a single page that details a single idea in your game and does this as succinctly as possible.

The idea is that you can put these one-pagers together as a sort of design mosaic, on a wall or other planning board, and everyone can refer to this as the whole of the game's design.

You can use **bold text** or ALL-CAPS to signify something like another one-pager to refer to. You can capitalize things like facts or pillars, or simply list them in a sidebar to highlight cases where they are particularly relevant. Every time you need to specify something, you write a one-pager for it.

Soon enough, you will have an accessible summary of your whole game design.

### Writing a One-Pager

1. Write a title for the one-pager's concept and add today's date. For the title, you can easily grab a Pillar, Feature, or Fact, from your design, or something that came up on another one-pager.

2. Note who the writer of the one-pager is and how to contact them. This shows ownership of the particular one-pager, if you have a team of designers.

3. Add a clear illustration of the concept you're describing. This serves to draw the eyes at a glance, and also to build a holistic view of the entire game when placed next to other one-pagers.

4. Write a single-paragraph description of what this one-pager is about. Large type, few words.

5. For details, add sidebars with bullet points that bring up the design of this one-pager. Each may refer to another one-pager or repeat a fact.

6. Add any illustrations or callouts you find relevant to elaborate on the one-pager's content in a visual way, for people who won't read the text at first glance.

7. If you want to get fancy, you can combine multiple one-pagers into larger wholes, for example as the four corners of a room detailing different features of the room.

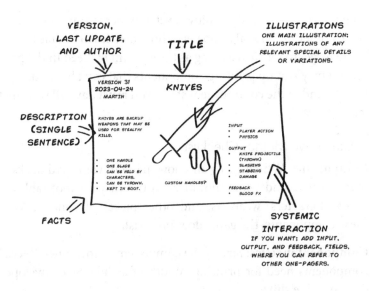

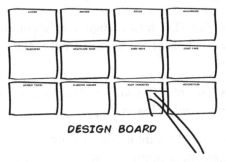

**DESIGN BOARD**
PUTTING ALL YOUR ONE-PAGERS TOGETHER SOMEWHERE GIVES YOU A GREAT VISUAL OVERVIEW OF THE WHOLE GAME'S DESIGN!

## SET METRICS

How high and wide a doorway is. How much gold a bowl of noodles costs. How many experience points you get from killing all the goblins in the goblin village for no apparent reason. How many cards there are in the deck of cards.

Balancing happens throughout the course of your development but setting baseline numbers for all the things in your game and making sure to store them in spreadsheets and/or databases, you can guarantee that nothing is forgotten or postponed. You can also make sure to set the structure in such a way that you can easily modify the numbers as you inevitably reach balancing. These may be metrics now, but in the future, they will be the levers and dials you must use to make the game behave the way you want.

Setting metrics also serves to allow level designers, component developers, and any other individuals who need those metrics to be able to do their jobs. If you forget to set such a thing as the amount of bleed in the printing process, you may end up printing components that can't be used.

Before the end of the commitment stage, you **must** have all your metrics in order.

A Non-Exhaustive Metrics Checklist

- **Components**: Which cards and how many in your card decks. How many entries and which numbers to use in your loot tables. How many characters, weapons, and other pieces of content. Without these components, the game does not exist.

- **Component metrics**: Size of the components. How much 'bleed' the components need for printing. Width of a shoe. Size envelope of a customizable shirt.

- **Gameplay metrics**: How far and high the player jumps. How fast the player moves. Goal play time or turn length. Number of cards you can play in a turn.

- **Level metrics**: Height and width of doorways, windows, and trapdoors. Footprints for level assets.

- **Character metrics**: Minimum and maximum heights and widths. Character counts. Maximum number of characters on-screen at any given time.

- **Technical metrics**: Maximum polycount per mesh. Skin weight influence per bone. Number of cards per print plate. Disk size limitations for game build distribution. Minimum spec for the target platform.

# SAMPLE METRICS

HEIGHT AND WIDTH OF
A 3D DOORWAY.

COMPONENT COUNTS.

VALUE OF IN-GAME
CURRENCY

LENGTH AND HEIGHT
OF A JUMP.

## PLAY, DON'T SHOW

Sometimes we think of the player's experience as something to direct and control.

The player comes in here, does this, and then goes over there. This can be exactly what we set out to do, a **cinematic** experience, but what works in film isn't necessarily the same as what works in games. This can be illustrated by extrapolating on the classic adage "show, don't tell." In games, it can be "play, don't show."

"[W]hen dealing with your narrative, create a priority for telling your story as follows: play it, display it, say it," writes Flint Dille and John Zuur Platten in their book *The Ultimate Guide to Video Game Writing and Design*. This is an effective checklist to use, since it reminds you that the main attraction of games is that they are interactive.

But whether to play or show is also an important commitment tool because knowing how you intend to present your game will preemptively resolve many potential issues in development.

If you want the game to be a cinematic experience as opposed to a systemic one, you must have decided this before you leave this stage of the design process. You must decide which parts of the game you will let players play, have the game display, or directly say.

### The Interactive Priority List

1. **Play it**: let the player make the thing happen.

2. **Display it**: show the event to the player.

3. **Say it**: state the event to the player.

### Practical Play, Don't Show Examples

If you are using any of the following techniques, you're *showing* the player something that they may instead be able to play.

- **Exposition cutscenes** explain story details that are external to the player and may not be obvious. Having the player play the scene instead both means you must scrutinize what you show and how you can make it compelling as an activity.

- **Scene direction** is when you take control of the camera to direct the player's attention to where they need to go or what they need to do. You can let the player discover this on their own, instead, by making sure that they will eventually have to go there once they have exhausted every other option.

- **Scene narration** is when you pull a lever and a cutscene shows you a door opening, or when a cutscene shows you that reinforcements are arriving. These things rarely need explanation—they can just be allowed to happen.

- **Control changes** are when a game normally allows certain actions but suddenly and arbitrarily takes the ability to perform those actions away.

- **Verbal or written directions** are the "go there," "fetch that," and "maybe you need to open the red door" that some designers call nag lines. Trusting the player to figure things out on their own can sometimes be a better way.

- **Visual directions** are in-game waypoint graphics and other cues that show you clearly where to go. The risk with these is that the player stops interacting with the game itself and only interacts with the user interface.

1) PLAY IT          2) DISPLAY IT          3) SAY IT

## CHECK IT

Make sure not to use trademarked or copyrighted terms, locations, *etc.* This may sound like a self-explanatory thing, but please—just look it up to see if it's taken.

For a layperson, the finer details of legislation can be extremely hard to predict. Even something that seems intuitive or like it couldn't possibly be misinterpreted can and will be misinterpreted. Even use of common words or axioms can get you in trouble if the same words and axioms are used by larger organizations with busy legal teams.

But this goes way beyond just legal ramifications. Considerations of representation, accessibility, and many other things are just as important—if not more so.

When you "check it," you make sure that as many people as possible can enjoy your game. You must of course consider which audiences are relevant, as well. If you are making a horror-themed game, it's probably not going to sell well to children anyway and you can probably safely ignore some age-based ratings restrictions.

This tool is the final gatekeeper before you commit to your game design. Ask yourself if you can do what you intend to do, but if you feel even an inkling of doubt, you should also ask yourself if you should.

Check Checklist

- **Trademarks with similar use of words**: This doesn't have to be the exact expression either. If you use onomatopoeia or common expressions, corporations with similar names may consider it a violation of their trademark.

- **Specific trademarks related to what you may think are common terms**: "Droid" is a registered trademark of Lucasfilm Entertainment Company Ltd., for example, and you can't use it for the robots in your game without a licensing agreement.

- **Cultural references with problematic local context**: Some countries may not want you to show the political symbols of their past, or they may ban your game because it uses harmful stereotypes or displays visible skeletons or human entrails. Global launch requires global awareness.

- **Ratings**: You can find guidelines for popular rating services online, and it's a good idea to keep track of what you can and can't do depending on your intended audience. Cursing and swearing can be limited, just like more graphical representations of violence may be restricted.

- **Triggers**: Some content is triggering and may require trigger warnings if you don't want to alienate certain audiences. Such trigger warnings apply to fear of spiders, fear of drowning, and many more.

- **Accessibility**: If you haven't considered it yet, you should look at accessibility before committing completely to your game. Making it possible to play your game even if you have some functional variation is a good way to reach a larger audience. At the very least, you should know who will have a hard time playing your game because of the design decisions you've made.

### CAN YOU? (LEGALLY, FINANCIALLY)

- *EXISTING TRADEMARKS OR COPYRIGHTS.*
- *OTHER GAMES THAT ARE TOO SIMILAR.*
- *REAL WORLD LOCATIONS OR LIKENESSES.*
- *COMPANY OR BRAND NAMES.*

### SHOULD YOU? (MORALLY, ETHICALLY)

- *OFFENSIVE OR TRIGGERING.*
- *ALIENATING CERTAIN AUDIENCES.*
- *INACCESSIBLE FEATURES.*
- *PAYGATED FEATURES.*

# CHAPTER 5

# Problem Solving

NOW YOU'RE COMMITTED AND know what your game is supposed to be when it's done. You can never go back to ideation or exploration at this point. It's time to get serious and ship your game. If you get cool ideas, by all means write them down somewhere, but they're not for this project.

Don't fear, however: design is still needed. Ideation and exploration aren't needed, but figuring out what to do when a button combination doesn't work or focus testers can't figure out where to go is very much needed. Besides, even if high-level iteration isn't happening anymore, you can still remove things from the game.

Solving real problems demonstrated by the playable game, even if it's in a rough state or only played by you and your close allies; that's what problem solving is all about.

What you do during problem solving:

- Play your game and have other people play your game all the time. Focus on finding problems and trying different solutions.

- Think about your customers and the personas that may describe them and try to picture what problems they would run into.

- Set up isolated focus tests and include Quality Assurance testing in your process, if you have the resources.

- In all likelihood, write a list of the problems you could live with if they were still there in your finished game.

DOI: 10.1201/9781003332756-6

## MAKE PLAYER PERSONAS

A "persona" is a made-up individual representing someone that would play your game. There are both guesstimated personas and personas sourced from extensive metrics. For the latter, NewZoo's *Gamer Segmentation and Gamer Personas* is a great starting point, available from NewZoo. For the former, you invent them as they're needed and to the best of your abilities.

Examining your game like these personas would is a good way to find problems to solve, as it may open your eyes to why a certain problem comes up or even warn you before it does. If you know that some players will only play 10 minutes per session, for example, and your game takes at least 15 minutes per session, you have a very clear and hopefully soluble problem right there.

You can think of a persona as a character made up for a role-playing game. It's an imaginary person modeled after real people and only serves its purpose if it's real enough to be convincing.

After making up a few personas, you look at how they would play your game differently from you and what kinds of problems come up when they do. You can then keep coming back to your library of personas and see how it causes new problems with your tweaked designs.

Making a Player Persona

- Write a brief bio—name, age, and profession—for your imagined persona. You may want to touch on social class, wealth, and other factors as well, depending on your game.

- Define how the persona interacts with games:

  - What was the first game they played?

  - Which platforms do they prefer playing on?

  - What hardware do they have access to?

  - How much money do they spend on gaming per month?

  - How much time do they commit to a new game on first play?

  - How many hours do they play per week?

  - Do they play mostly multiplayer, mostly single-player, or a mix of both?

- Do they have a regular board- or role-playing group they play with?

- Do they play mostly online games?

- Do they play many kinds of games, or stick to specific genres, or even a single game?

- Do they play games or mostly watch streams of other people playing, or both?

- Explore how the persona would interact with your game, based on the information you have provided.

- Explore if you could do something to make the game more viable for them, or if you have to accept them as a "lost cause," and what that means for your design. If a certain type of player is unlikely to play your game in the first place, there may be concessions you made earlier that you can unmake.

- Play the game as you imagine the persona would, faster, slower or more carefully or recklessly. Use the persona to vary your own play style and make sure to note any problems that come up that will need solving.

| YOUNG GAMER | [A]GE GAMER | OLD GAMER |
|---|---|---|
| SPENDS BOTH MONEY AND TIME PLAYING GAMES AND PREFERS PLAYING COMPETITIVE GAMES. HAS LOTS OF TIME BUT LIMITED DISPOSABLE INCOME. | [INT]ERESTS BESIDES GAMING. [KE]EPS PLAYING GAMES. BOTH [AN]D ONLINE, [SAM]E FRIENDS AS BEFORE. | HAS DISPOSABLE INCOME, BUT MOSTLY PURCHASES OLD BIG-BOX GAMES ON ONLINE AUCTIONS. BUYS MANY GAMES, BUT HAS LITTLE TIME TO PLAY |
| FIRST GAME? FORTNITE | [CALL] OF DUTY | FIRST GAME? ELITE |
| PLATFORMS? PHONE AND CONSOLE | [C]ONSOLE | PLATFORMS? ALL OF THEM |
| HOURS PER WEEK? 10 - 30 | [WEE]K? 10 - 20 | HOURS PER WEEK? 1 - 5 |
| WATCHES STREAMS? YES, SEVERAL | [STREAM]S? YES, AND NOT ONLY GAMING STREAMS. | WATCHES STREAMS? YES, DUE TO LIMITED PLAYTIME. |

## OBSERVE AND ANALYZE

One of the very first things you should do when your game can be played is watch people play it. This is equally true for all kinds of games. By removing yourself from the game but not the play test you will see how easy (or hard) your game is to understand and you'll learn things you could never have anticipated.

The hardest part of this observation is that you are likely to want to tell your testers what to do when they get things wrong. But it's absolutely essential for the process that you don't succumb to this temptation. The moment you start explaining things, you have ruined the observations you could've made.

If you ask questions, you must ask them in a way that doesn't guide the player and you shouldn't ask anything at all until after the play session is complete. It can be tempting to ask, "what do you think the button to the right does?", because you desperately want them to press it, but you shouldn't. If they're not pressing that button, there may be a problem with your design.

Just hover around the players and take in as much as you can. Or use one of those one-way mirrors that are always used in interrogation scenes in the movies, if you have access to one. Or just make sure to record the play session so you can watch it later.

Lastly, never use a single test observation as the basis for a design decision. Bring in more testers to see if the takeaways can be made more consistently. The more tests, the better.

### Observer's Checklist and Follow-Up Questions

- Note where they get stuck. *Ask if there were places or situations where they felt stuck.*

- Note what they do wrong or misinterpret. *Ask them what they were trying to make happen, and why—don't imply that anything was wrong.*

- Note which features they use a lot. *Ask them which things they liked and which they didn't like, and why, but don't ask about specific features. Let them mention the features.*

- Note which features they don't use at all. *Ask them which things they didn't like, and why, but again don't imply that you mean anything specific.*

- Note if there are things they choose to skip or avoid. *Ask them about skipping and avoiding; be careful not to imply what they may have skipped since it can also be an honest mistake.*

- Note any unexpected behavior that you had not foreseen when you designed or made the features. *This is both for discovery, meaning finding cool things you didn't expect, and for resolving potential issues with the game's presentation. If players are somehow encouraged to do things you don't want them to, you need to figure out why.*

- Finally, after the test is finished and you have asked any other questions, ask the play testers more generally if there are things they would've changed, and if so, what, how, and why. *This should be the last question, or some types of testers will get "stuck" on their own ideas in their head.*

## TEST BLIND

A blind test is when you send your build or prototype to someone who doesn't know you and has no connection to your project. Since everyone is (at least) a Level 1 designer, this type of testing is highly valuable since it completely removes your own personal creator's bias from the test data. The drawback is of course that you can't always observe the play session directly.

Testers who test blindly will have to learn the game just like any other first-time player who buys your game and are therefore valuable test subjects. Unlike many other play tests, where you are present to explain the game or help out (against better judgment) when someone gets stuck, a blind test excludes any input you may have that affects the test result.

Ideally, the test can be recorded and shared with you so you can hear the players talk about their session and look at how they engage with the game. If that's not possible for some reason, the second-best way is to have everyone fill out a form with non-leading questions so you can know what they felt about it.

In many board game design communities and indie developer communities, blind testing each other's games is done quid pro quo. "You test mine and I'll test yours." If you have the luxury of being part of such a community, get as much testing in as you possibly can. But make sure to give back at least as much as you get.

Things to Look for in Blind Tests

- **Teaching**: If players can get into the game at the speed you are hoping for, as well as any specific hurdles they run into along the way.

- **Basic understanding**: If players are doing the right thing at the right time or missing out on something important.

- **Session length**: For how long players play, and at what points in your game they seem to trail off. Use a timer with board games and similar. With digital games, you can track player attrition using analytics; for example, by sending data to a database at the end of every level or at regular intervals.

- **Off-hand comments**: When you're not there, and people don't know you, what they say about the game will usually be much more honest and to the point. They may even openly criticize some design decisions you've made. This stuff is invaluable, and in many ways the best part of blind tests. Listen carefully and take it all in.

- **Reactions**: If you have recordings, looking at how people react at certain moments in the game is also invaluable, for example, when they draw the cool overpowered card, or when they fall into an opponent's trap. If you see things that surprise you, that's great. If you see what you hoped for, that's also great. It means that your game is working as intended!

- **"The game"** *vs* **"Me"**: One thing that's worth listening for is when people talk about what they did *vs* what the game did. It's common for good things to be "me," and bad things to be "the game," giving you relevant clues to pick up on.

## DRAW A STRATEGY MAP

When your design allows many different solutions or strategies, it's easy to forget some of them because you've become closely acquainted with others. You may also have avoided some strategies because the components weren't finished or they hadn't been implemented yet. Even once they're there, you may forget to use them.

In all cases where you have multiple alternative routes to reach goals or to end a game, you need to verify that they all work and that they are all engaging your players.

Enter the strategy map! A strategy map lists all the viable strategies for a given situation in your game and provides ways to check if they are all getting sufficient attention.

For example, if you have a game with two different victory conditions, a strategy map can show all the different intended ways to reach each of them. The strategies that are available to the player.

By documenting each play test—your own or someone else's—you can then note which victory condition was triggered and which strategy was used. If 90% of sessions end because of the same strategy, it means that the other strategies are underrepresented and that you need to tweak the game to make the underused strategies more interesting.

If you have a game where combat and parkour are important features, for example, but only the parkour is seeing consistent use, you may need to ramp up the combat or even consider whether the combat should be there at all.

A strategy map is a reminder of how you want the game to be played, and a simple way to verify that you have covered your bases.

General Strategy Map

- List any relevant starting conditions, including the outcomes of any initial choices players need to make. *Starting faction, weapon, location, etc.*

- List the game's end conditions. *Player character killed, deck runs out of cards, Rome is invaded by barbarians, etc.*

- Going backward from each end condition, list the choices or events that lead to them, until you arrive at the starting conditions and complete the map.

- Keep each choice broad. List just a few steps per strategy.

- You don't have to list every conceivable action the game allows, only the high level strategies that are expected to lead to interesting pivots in the game.

- It's okay to have the arrows you draw meet at places where certain choices would lead to the same outcomes.

- It's also fine if some strategies require more steps than others. This in itself isn't necessarily a problem as the steps may vary in complexity.

## Reinforcement Checks

Once you have a strategy map, you can use it to verify both that the strategies are created equal and that the activities themselves reinforce the game you are making. For example:

- **Personality checks**: Using the map to check that the activities are something that the main character would do.

- **Brand checks**: Making sure each activity in the strategy map reinforces the brand you are working on.

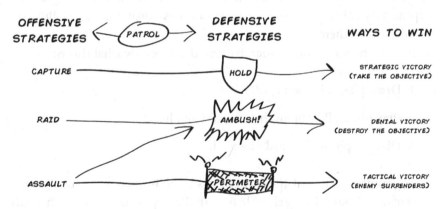

A STRATEGY MAP REMINDS YOU OF THE END CONDITIONS
AND THE DIFFERENT WAYS FOR PLAYERS TO REACH THEM.

## VERIFY WITH CHECKLISTS

It's easy to get lost while making a game. You start the game already knowing everything that should happen. You get used to the red icons in the log that tell you something went wrong, or you browse past your notes on what to fix in the game rules. Your muscle memory goes through the main menu so fast that you don't even take note of the misspelled words or the options that are now broken.

Sometimes repetition or even some kind of fatigue settles in, and you can't really see the game for what it is anymore. You can't see the forest for the trees, as the proverb goes.

At times like these, it's good to have checklists ready to make you remember how the game is supposed to work. This isn't about strategies however, there is a key difference here. These checklists need to be here to remind you of the repetitive stuff you don't think about—strategy maps are there to make sure that you are giving players what you want them to have.

These checklists can also help you with the design work itself and will inform new coworkers, potential play testers, and others on how to play your game.

### Action Checklists

An action or feature interaction checklist is probably the most self-explanatory thing you will ever have to do as a game designer. But you should still do them.

Picture the classic turn order list, and that's exactly what this is:

1. **Draw phase**: Draw a card.

2. **Play phase**: Play up to three cards from hand.

3. **Discard phase**: Discard one card.

How granular you want these checklists to be is a factor of your game's level of detail, but making checklists of all the steps you have to go through to make standard tasks like changing the resolution or looking up which button to press will keep you focused throughout your game's delivery and make sure that any big changes can be spotted more easily.

It's also a good way to find where steps may be simplified or even removed.

## CHANGING SCREEN RESOLUTION

☐ LAUNCH THE GAME

☐ WATCH THROUGH THE TITLE SEQUENCE

☐ WAIT FOR THE INTRO CINEMATIC TO END

☐ PRESS ANY BUTTON ON THE START MENU

☐ CLICK OR PRESS "SETTINGS"

☐ CLICK OR PRESS "GRAPHICS"

☐ CLICK OR PRESS "DISPLAY RESOLUTION"

☐ PICK YOUR DESIRED RESOLUTION

☐ CLICK OR PRESS "APPLY"

☐ IF PROMPTED TO VERIFY,
CLICK OR PRESS "YES" OR "NO."

## PLAYING A TURN

☐ CHECK IF YOU WIN

☐ IF YOU DON'T WIN, DRAW THREE CARDS

☐ ON EACH CARD, RESOLVE ANY
"PLAY IMMEDIATELY" EFFECTS

☐ PLAY AS MANY CARDS AS YOU CAN

☐ END YOUR TURN

SOME CHECKLISTS MAY NOT SEE
THAT MUCH USE. BUT KEEP THEM AROUND.
OUR ABILITY TO FORGET IMPORTANT
THINGS IS REMARKABLE!

THESE CHECKLISTS CAN ALSO
HELP YOU ELIMINATE STEPS FROM
UNNECESSARILY COMPLEX INTERACTIONS.

## VALIDATE YOUR PILLARS

The "Crate Review System" was created by the website *Old Man Murray* in the early 2000s. It's a tongue in cheek feature that lists some popular games at the time and scores them based on how many seconds passed before the player saw a wooden crate, barrel, or other crate-like object. The score is referred to as "seconds to crate." The higher the better, since it would seemingly imply greater imagination from the developers.

Setting aside that this would remain an accurate review system still to this day, the principle of using scoring to determine problems with your game design is something you can also apply. It can be used to review your own work and to make sure you're living up to your claims by setting up concrete measurable validation tests.

The trickiest part of design validation is to avoid false positives and false negatives. With the many ways we can use analytics software in modern digital games, for example, or build elaborate spreadsheets, the statistics generated can easily be used in a selective way. This destroys the benefits of said data.

The best way to avoid these false results is to use data that's concrete and doesn't provide room for speculation. Time and other crisp numbers, like the number of kills, cards drawn, or game turns. Any data that won't leave room for interpretation and can be easily actionable. Counting seconds is one of the most effective ones, since you can easily check if future changes add or subtract seconds from the new results. But any number that can be directly compared between gameplay iterations can be used.

### Example Design Validation Checks

- **Seconds to kill:** If you want a more intense action game, measuring the number of seconds from splash screen to first kill is an effective tool. It forces you to reconsider login screens and other pre-game processes. It can of course be applied to other actions besides killing; Seconds to Jump, Seconds to Build, Seconds to Card Draw, and so on.

- **Seconds per kill:** Another interesting metric for action is to measure how many seconds each enemy survives in the simulation. This number can go down to 3–5 seconds in some styles of action games and may go up toward an hour in a particularly daunting boss fight. As with Seconds to Kill, this can be applied to other interactions too.

- **Session length:** If you set a target at 5 minutes, and the game takes shorter or longer to play, you need to figure out ways to tune session length by adding or removing choices, content, or friction.

- **Turn count:** To check how long your game is, in a turn-based game, you can measure the total number of turns being played each session. A full session of Civilization 6 is said to average to around 500 turns.

- **Turn length:** With turns, you can also measure how long each individual turn takes to complete, taking into account that players play differently.

- **Two-hour test:** For reasons of Steam's return policy, a common validation test is the Two-Hour Test, where you want your game to be played for a minimum of 2 hours before a player drops out.

- **Player turnover:** Checking how many players leave before finishing the game and seeing if you can change that trend by tweaking the design.

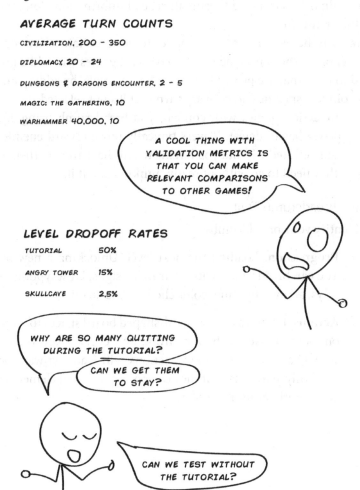

**AVERAGE TURN COUNTS**

CIVILIZATION, 200 – 350

DIPLOMACY 20 – 24

DUNGEONS & DRAGONS ENCOUNTER, 2 – 5

MAGIC: THE GATHERING, 10

WARHAMMER 40,000, 10

A COOL THING WITH VALIDATION METRICS IS THAT YOU CAN MAKE RELEVANT COMPARISONS TO OTHER GAMES!

**LEVEL DROPOFF RATES**

TUTORIAL        50%

ANGRY TOWER     15%

SKULLCAVE       2.5%

WHY ARE SO MANY QUITTING DURING THE TUTORIAL?

CAN WE GET THEM TO STAY?

CAN WE TEST WITHOUT THE TUTORIAL?

## LAY A TRAIL

Sometimes, players simply don't get it. They must turn that corner to get to the next stage of the level but seem unwilling to do so, or they somehow forget to flip the card over in their hand and therefore miss the information they need.

This is where a trail can be useful—just like Hansel leaving a trail of breadcrumbs to find the way back home. In honor of that particular fairytale, you can refer to this tool as "breadcrumbing."

If you have a goal that the player needs to reach, you lay a trail along the way to that goal.

The breadcrumbs of the trail can be spinning gold coins to pick up, biscuits to eat, boulders to break, treasure chests to open, or something else. In many board game designs, the physical board acts as a trail, where you can only move to a certain location by following a specified path. The player is almost guaranteed to gain all crucial information along the way, from the board itself.

It can still be useful to add incentives to go to certain places or make certain choices, the way some role-based board games will add a growing reward to roles that are picked less often. For example, by adding an additional coin to a specific choice every turn that it's not selected.

In many action games with combat, you breadcrumb using enemies that the player has to defeat. Players typically move toward enemies that haven't been defeated without you having to tell them and are then guided to where they need to go without really thinking about it.

Laying a Breadcrumb Trail

- Identify your breadcrumbs:

  - **Progression**: Loading the next level. Unlocking a new feature. You can breadcrumb with clear EXIT signs, UI waypoints, doorways, arrows, lighting, color choices, and so on.

  - **Actions**: Enemies to fight, card-shaped board spaces to play cards on, bouncy pads to bounce from, and checkboxes to check on your character sheet. Many actions will lead the way forward smoothly, particularly if they can be tied to visual elements in the game world or user interface.

- **Incentives**: Coins, ammunition, collectables, extra card draws, and treasures; all of you who ever played a 3D game and looked under a stair to find some extra ammo have been "breadcrumbed" there by the promise of juicy pickups.

- Figure out where you want the player to go or which choices you want the player to make that they aren't making.

- Add breadcrumbs toward these choices:

  - First, use **Incentives**, since they are less disruptive and more gently guide the player. It's a tentative promise more than handholding.

  - Second, use **Actions**. Things the player will be doing anyway, except now you use it to guide them forward. The risk of doing this too much is that the breadcrumbing becomes too obvious or the action tedious.

  - Thirdly, use **Progression** breadcrumbs. If nothing else works, this may be your only option. But it's the last option because it risks diminishing the player's personal sense of discovery.

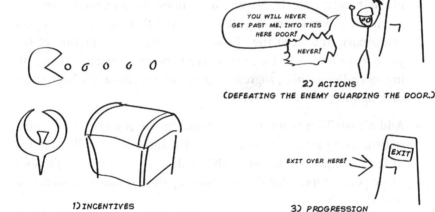

YOU WILL NEVER GET PAST ME, INTO THIS HERE DOOR!

NEVER!

**2) ACTIONS**
(DEFEATING THE ENEMY GUARDING THE DOOR.)

EXIT OVER HERE!  EXIT

**1) INCENTIVES**
(TREASURES, PICKUPS, BISCUITS, ETC.)

**3) PROGRESSION**
(COMPLETION AND END CONDITIONS.)

## MAKE IT ESCALATE

I attack; you block. You attack; I block.

Two action sequences with exactly no results to their name except maybe some suspense. There could've been a million action sequences of the same repeated exchange and nothing would ever happen. We'll stand there taking turns to attack and block until we get bored and quit the game.

An exchange where the sum total of game resources doesn't change can be referred to as a "zero-sum" exchange. It's zero-sum because one person's gain is equal to another person's loss. It is something that easily leads to an uninteresting back-and-forth.

You generally don't want zero-sum exchanges in your gameplay interactions. Instead, you want to escalate your scenes, making them cost or generate resources in order to build toward a compelling outcome. Making something happen that builds forward momentum and ensures that the game always feels like it's going somewhere.

This is where the stamina bars, ammunition counters, countdown timers, and many other designs come from. They make the game escalate, constantly moving toward a lose condition that the player can only avoid by engaging with the game.

Escalate!

- **Make it scale**: Give the player a sense of escalation from the system. From their own improving skills allowing them to manage higher complexity, and from the visual or physical representation of the game. For example by having them roll one die at first and then rolling more dice as they progress. Fighting one enemy at the beginning; then fighting 100 near the end.

- **Add a cost**: To mix up the pace, there can be costs or diminishing returns to repetitive actions. Think of mana to cast spells, stamina to keep making attacks, or gradually decreasing ammo or durability on your weapon that forces you to repair it, reload it, or switch to something else.

- **Add a gain**: Adding more resources into the simulation will give the side that accumulates most of it an upper hand. If the gain is something that can be contested, like randomly appearing powerups or card draws, it also creates incentive for players to get at the resource before others do.

- **Add choices**: Escalation can also be turned into a player choice. Which weapon to use; which distance to engage at; when to switch from stealth to combat; how to time the micro nuke; when to use your "play at any time" counter card.

- **Allow finishing moves**: Some games allow players to gradually accumulate resources that allow them not just to escalate but to push directly for an ending. A finishing move is victorious—whatever that means for your game.

- **Allow retreat**: The opposite of a finishing move. As the player takes a first tentative step onto the rope bridge and hears the ominous creaking, they can decide to not put their weight down and go find another way. Or, as they see the resource competition turn against them, they can leave to fight another day.

**THIS COULD GO ON FOREVER:**

**UNLESS IT SOMEHOW ESCALATES:**

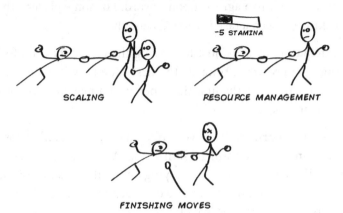

SCALING

RESOURCE MANAGEMENT

FINISHING MOVES

## GIVE THEM CARROTS

If you forget to have breakfast in some survival games, you starve to death before lunch. It is hardly a fun experience for a player struggling to scavenge berries while learning the controls.

Similarly, a player may never have used the card drawing ability of their character and feel like they never have enough cards as a result. This becomes a problem for your game because it means that players won't have fun, and they are highly likely to blame the game for this.

Some games feel too punishing, or you can't get players to engage with what you think are the game's coolest features. This is an excellent opportunity to reach for the carrots, rewarding the player's success instead of punishing their failure.

In the survival game example, it could be by changing it from having starvation cause death to make the player benefit from having eaten, for example by gaining extra experience points, moving faster, or something similar.

In the card game, it can simply be that you get to draw more cards if you play more cards, for example, by letting you always draw up to a set number of cards at the start of your turn.

Add Carrots

- **Boosting**: Few players must be convinced to grab powerups when they find them. These are the things that make them move faster, deal more damage, gain more points, draw more cards, *etc*. A booster of some kind is an efficient carrot. Compare eating to gain more points to eating so you don't take damage from starvation.

- **Completion awards**: Repeat a certain action or activity a number of times to gain an agreed-upon reward. For some players, the act of checking off such a task is reward enough.

- **Participation awards**: Just for having the player show up for something, you provide a reward. The first time they use a feature, they gain something or the first time they visit a new location or enter a new board space.

- **Consolation prizes**: When you come in last, or you fail to complete a task in time, you can still get something. A consolation prize. At best, this will teach players to keep trying and will take some of the stress away from failure. But it can also devalue the sense of achievement in overcoming a challenge, so it must be used carefully.

- **Random rewards**: In describing the psychology of operant conditioning, B.F. Skinner writes, "we make a given consequence contingent on certain physical properties of behavior […], and the behavior is then observed to increase in frequency." That is to say, if we provide you a consistent reward for physical behavior, you will engage in that behavior more. This is one area where random rewards are often used in games. Loot drops, card draws, and treasure chests. If you fail motivating your players in other ways, handing out random rewards may be the last resort. For many players, it's the juiciest carrot.

**BOOSTING**
*INCENTIVIZE CERTAIN ACTIONS BY HAVING THEM MAKE OTHER ACTIONS MORE EFFECTIVE.*

**COMPLETION**
*REWARDS FOR FINISHING SOMETHING.*

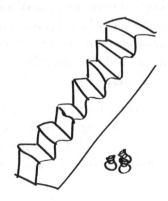

**CONSOLATION PRIZES**
*WE DON'T WANT YOU TO LOOK UNDER THE STAIRS, BUT NOW THAT YOU DID, HERE'S SOME STUFF!*

## BURN THEM ON THE STOVE

You tell children not to put their hand on the proverbial stove. When they inevitably do so anyway, they learn the hard way why they shouldn't, and this reinforces your message much more than any amount of nagging could ever do.

This can be just as effective for teaching players what to do by clearly demonstrating what they should avoid. First tell them what they shouldn't do, and then once they do it anyway you give them a lasting "pain:" you burn them on the stove.

As long as this effect is clearly and consistently triggered by the same behavior, players will learn to avoid it. Maybe even practice avoiding it, turning it into a skill element in your game.

In some types of games, where the loops are clearly directed and players have to perform certain actions in a certain order, this can be referred to as "learning by dying." Until you complete the desired loop, any actions you do out of sequence will kill you and reset the game state for you to try again.

Many of the single-player *Call of Duty* games use this kind of teaching, as does the popular *Dark Souls* series but in a very different way.

Maybe the clearest example of "learning by dying" is in games like *Hotline Miami*, where the pace is extremely fast and you will enter a stage, try one approach, die, try another approach, and continue doing so until you succeed. (Or quit.)

Add Stoves

- **Stuns**: Any effect that temporarily disables you is in effect a "stun." It can be losing a turn in a board game, having to walk back to your corpse in a Massively Multiplayer Online Role-Playing Game to respawn, getting blinded momentarily, or having your weapon overheat from repeated use, *etc.*

- **Hindering**: A hindrance is a negative effect—the inverse of a boost—that causes you some lasting annoyance until you do what you are expected to do to get rid of it. Moving more slowly, vision blurrier, playing with fewer cards on hand, having your input controls inverted, *etc.*

- **Feature denial:** This is having one of your standard features punished if you use it. Discard a card, take some damage, and fall down; whatever you can come up with, it's triggered by using the feature that is currently denied to you. The feature may still work and then have this effect on top of it, or it can be replaced entirely by the denial effect.

- **Feature loss:** Complete loss of a certain feature is another way of burning players on the stove. Removing the ability to sprint because you carry too much stuff, for example, or making it impossible to attack if you exhausted all your remaining stamina.

- **Reversal:** Teach the player that something they often do is a good thing, and then suddenly punish them for it. The classic *Dungeons & Dragons* mimic is maybe the best example of this type of reversal. Adventurers always run to treasure chests in search of gold—then suddenly one treasure chest bites their arm off! Every future treasure chest will be shot with an arrow before it's opened.

## SOLVE PROBLEMS

Apologies for stating the obvious in a chapter on problem solving, but this is a very important reminder to not get caught in minutiae.

If you find yourself in long-winded discussions that seem to lead nowhere, ask yourself "what problems are we solving right now?" If there's no clear answer, table the discussion and move on. By this time in a project's lifecycle, you shouldn't be engaged in freeform brainstorming anymore. That's why this reminder is important.

If you're not solving a problem, and you're no longer ideating or exploring, chances are that your discussion isn't worth having. This is a great risk with every kind of creative endeavor, and it can sometimes feel demeaning to be told that the discussion you're trying to have isn't worth having, but the faster you can reach the mindset of "what problems are we solving right now?" the less time will be wasted.

There are three specific areas where this is especially important.

**Writers** can come up with ideas that have large-scale ramifications in the time it takes to form a thought and commit it to paper. Whether changing the scope of the project or taking it into an unexplored direction, these changes must be kept in check.

**Artists** can do the same, particularly sketch artists and concept artists, where a quick hand can invent something compelling in the space of a few seconds.

Lastly, **game designers**; probably the most consistent offenders when it comes to thinking up new things that affect large-scale changes. But if you keep doing this by this point in a project, you've decided to stay at Level 1. We don't need any of the Level 1 game designer shenanigans right now. Not for this project! Get back to solving problems.

Ask, "What Problems Are We Solving?" When…

- …you are discussing something that has no tangible feature or in-game content connected to it.

- …you are working on texts or even whole documents where none of the material is player-facing.

- …you start discussing things that concern plot, characters, levels, fundamental board redesigns, or other elements of the game that are expensive to do, too late to consider, or practically unlikely to actually happen.

- ...you start talking about cool things in the most recent blockbuster game and how you could maybe do those things in your game too.

- ...you bring up subjects that would affect things drastically, and the owners of said work are not even part of the conversation.

- ...you return to a subject that's important to someone personally but not what you are actually supposed to talk about right now.

- ...you get too caught up in anecdotes, supposition, arbitrary extrapolation, or other most likely irrelevant sidetracks. Note that any statement about what players may want, without evidence from playtesting, is exactly this.

- ...you start talking about things you may or may not want to do in the future that doesn't concern the game you're actually currently working on.

## LEAVE THINGS BEHIND

Sometimes, something crops up as a problem over and over again. It doesn't feel right, it's not fun, and it gets bad feedback consistently. It's clear that something's off with this thing. But you still feel like it's a key feature that needs to stay, because it's been with you since the beginning, or because at its core it's a nice feature.

Try playing your game without this thing. If it's a massive subsystem with interconnected parts, it can be tricky to do that play test, but make sure to do it. Then play without the feature for a while before coming back to the conversation again.

There's a bigger chance than you think that the system or feature simply doesn't belong in your game and that the best course of action is to leave it behind.

But there's a reason we're saying that you're leaving it behind and not simply deleting it.

Every time you leave a feature behind you expand your library of potentially awesome future gameplay features. With more time, they will mature, and you may figure out ways to solve the problems the feature had in the past. Or you may discover a new technical solution or complementary feature that allows it to make more sense and get even better.

So please—leave things behind. Do it more than you think you should. Ideas only get better with time.

### When to Leave Things Behind

- When multiple features provide the same function, you can leave one of them behind, unless you can differentiate it enough to make it relevant.

- When you are arguing for a specific feature from your perspective as a designer, and not for the benefit of the player, and you find no other reasons for the feature's existence in the current game than your own vanity, you should most definitely leave it behind. As a Level 3 or 4 designer, your intuition may very well be worth listening to in cases like this. But even then, vanity isn't a great reason to keep features around.

- When the thing you are arguing for doesn't fit the theme or represents something players will not want to do in this particular game, you can safely leave it behind. The cooking side mission in your chess game maybe sounds brilliant and could be a whole game in its own right, but let's focus on the chess for now.

- When the feature is something you've kept in the game because it was intended to solve a problem, but the problem has been solved in other ways by now, then you can leave the old solution behind. Before you had the wings in, you added the really long midair dash. With the wings in place, maybe the dash should go.

- When a feature is completely isolated from other features, only serving a single narrow purpose, it can be worth reevaluating and possibly leaving behind. If there's just one single place in your giant open world game where you make use of the special physics-driven rope ladder, it may not be worth the debugging effort to keep it.

# CHAPTER 6

# Balancing

THE GAME FUNDAMENTALLY WORKS by now but isn't quite ready for the mass market. It should be ready for your fans and for fans of similar games, however. Ready for more careful scrutiny.

This is where you can do beta testing or something like it. Discuss the project in forums, at conferences, or developer meetups, if you have the luxury of an existing community.

After having solved problems for a while, you already know all the sliders and variables and spreadsheet details you have to work with. Then comes the more fine-grained process of balancing all of it into a cohesive and compelling whole.

You're still playing and watching others play but you do so to observe the results of your balancing. It's the game design equivalent of visual polish.

Balancing serves a number of purposes:

- Getting the whole game to a playable state that communicates to everyone what the game is about and what it's like to play: no longer just in theory.

- Trimming away unnecessary features.

- Toning things down that are too extreme.

- Toning things up that aren't extreme enough.

- Polishing how synergies and features are communicated to players.

DOI: 10.1201/9781003332756-7

## ONE THING AT A TIME

Before we get into more practical tools related to balancing, there's a major thing that requires mentioning: focus. There's a paradox in balancing that goes something like this: **the easiest thing in balancing is to get the results you want; the hardest thing in balancing is to understand how**.

What often ends up happening is that we change many things at the same time, and it gets impossible to say which change it was that actually made things better. Particularly if there are multiple people trying to effect the same change in different ways.

If we feel combat is too fast, for example, we may decrease weapon damage, increase enemy health, change the effective range of weapons, tweak the amount of ammo you have available, alter the multiplier applied by a hit to the enemy's head, and so on. But what happens if we do all those changes at once is that we have no idea which change actually made the combat feel better. We achieved our result, but we don't know how.

Because of this, you need to tread lightly with balancing changes and focus on one thing at a time.

### Retaining Focus

When you balance things, stick to making **one change in one area** and then testing it.

The following are the areas that typically need balancing:

- **Data**: change the 1 into a 2, or the color red to blue. Data are often the easiest thing to change, and a good development pipeline will allow you to make changes in bulk. For example, "double the damage for all weapons" or "halve the health for all enemies."

- **System**: make changes to the flow of data. Where it's used as input, where it comes from as output, and how it generates feedback to players. It's important to separate this from the data, however. If you change how the data are used, you shouldn't also make changes to the data. Think of system as the rules that govern your game. If you are changing the rules, you are changing the system, and then you shouldn't also change the data.

- **Content**: replace whole cards or decks, tweak 3D models, make changes to level design, and make other more extensive changes that usually take longer to perform and test. They may also require the support of specialists like artists or level designers. As with the other changes, if you make changes to content—don't change data or systems at the same time, unless you must because of how things are linked together.

- **Removal**: anything you would change in the previous areas you can also simply remove and try without. Removing systems you know work can help you narrow your focus to exactly the tweaks that make the biggest difference. But it can also make you forget the intricacies of the complete game, so you must do so carefully.

PLAYER
ATTACK DAMAGE: 20
ATTACK SPEED: 1

PLAYER
ATTACK DAMAGE: 40
ATTACK SPEED: 10

GOBLINS CAN TAKE TOO MUCH DAMAGE!

MULTIPLY ATTACK SPEED BY 10
DOUBLE DAMAGE

HALVE GOBLIN HEALTH
REMOVE GOBLIN ARMOR

WHY ARE THE GOBLINS DYING SO FAST?!

GOBLIN
HEALTH: 100
ARMOR: 10

GOBLIN
HEALTH: 50
ARMOR: 0

## ASK SLY QUESTIONS

On one particular project, which was a cooperative first-person shooter, we had some strict limitations. These limitations dictated that there could be no more than eight active enemies at any given time.

At first, this seemed restrictive. It seemed like players would quickly get bored with so few enemies to interact with. But when we played it ourselves, we never felt like it was a problem. Not after we'd made the game interesting to play under the circumstances.

The lead designer came up with a way to test it. Rather than asking what we wanted to know— "is eight enemies too few?"—they asked testers, "how many enemies were you fighting at a time?"

With the fast pacing of the game (measured as how many seconds the average enemy was alive), answers from players were all across the chart. Most would answer that there were around 12–15 enemies, but some answered as many as 30 (!).

This made it clear that how you ask a question is highly relevant. Our fear that eight would be too few was simply unfounded, because players felt like there were many more.

Asking questions in a way that the answer informs you of things that are seemingly unrelated is an art form, but one you will need to practice a lot as a game designer. The moment you start asking explicitly, you will often lose the most relevant answers.

Sly Questions

- Ask play testers how things feel as opposed to how they think things work. If possible, tie these questions directly to problems you think you may have or that have been reported by other play testers, just like the example with the limited number of enemies.

- Ask play testers where they were going rather than why they got lost. Implying that a play tester did something wrong may sometimes affect the result, because they'll try to remedy their "mistakes" in their answers. It's better to let them describe what happened, how, and why, with you as a neutral inquirer.

- Give play testers choices rather than asking them open questions. Keep the choices succinct and specific.

  - **A/B questions:** "Do you think the main character is cool? Yes/ No."

- **Commentary**: "About the main character, what makes you feel that way?" Note here: avoid "if you said yes, then what makes you feel that way," for the same reason of neutrality mentioned earlier.

- **Graded questions**: "On a scale of 1–10, how would you rate this game's pacing? 1 = Really slow, 5 = Average, 10 = Really fast." The tricky thing with point grades is that higher values will imply a better answer, and that's not always desirable. Be careful with what you imply with your high grades.

- **Last thoughts**: "Any last thoughts about the main character you want to share?" should be separated from, "Any last thoughts about the game's pacing?" Just for clarity. Only ask these types of questions if you have concerns about some area of your game.

## AVOID DOMINATION

Sometimes, you'll see players use the same feature constantly, and it's fine. You'd never disallow the drawing of cards in a card game, for example. That'd just be silly. But sometimes it's because other features are not as good or because the specific feature is too good.

There are two cases where this is a problem (borrowed from the concept of strategic dominance in game theory):

The first is called a **dominant strategy**, where one strategy always leads to better results. There's no need for walking if you have an unlimited sprint you can use—next to walking, sprinting becomes the dominant strategy for moving faster.

The second is a **dominated strategy**, where something is simply so much worse than the other things that no one uses it. There's no need to use the single-shot pistol once you have a pistol with a magazine, maybe, making shooting with the single-shot pistol a dominated strategy.

There are cases where domination can be something you want. If that first gun is an iconic weapon that defines the character using it, then maybe it should be a dominant choice because the player will be using it throughout the entire game.

In *Marvel's Spider-Man*, web-slinging is definitely a dominant choice when compared to walking, for example. This is entirely by design. You only need to avoid domination when it makes your game less interesting or doesn't fit the game's premise.

### Eliminating Dominant Strategies

- **Save it for later**: If you need to keep it as-is for whatever reason, postpone access to the dominant strategy to a later stage of the game. This doesn't remove its dominance but makes it more of a reward akin to a powerup.

- **Add rules restrictions**: Maybe the dominant strategy can only be employed under certain circumstances. A stealthy kill in a *Hitman* game, for example, that can only be performed easily when the enemy is unaware of the player's avatar, Agent 47.

- **Add usage restrictions**: Maybe the dominant strategy can only be used once, costs a significant number of resources to use, or triggers a dangerous avalanche on use. Having to consider usage beyond the immediate gain will make the strategy less dominant.

Eliminating Dominated Strategies

- **Add a resource advantage**: Maybe this type of fuel isn't great, but it's abundant. You can find it almost anywhere, and lots of it. Making the less favored option more abundant or even unlimited makes it a safe fallback more than a dominated option.

- **Add niche protection**: Maybe the single-shot pistol isn't all that great, but later in the game it turns out it's the only weapon that can harm werewolves. Suddenly it's the one-shot werewolf pistol and its use is no longer a dominated strategy.

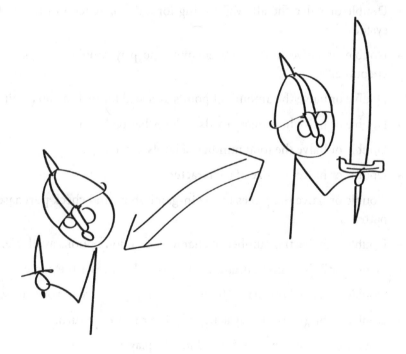

**DOMINANT**
BIG COOL SWORD:
DOES LOTS OF DAMAGE AND REACHES FAR.

- SAVE IT FOR THE LATE GAME.
- ADD RULES RESTRICTIONS: ENEMY SKELETONS ARE IMMUNE!
- ADD USAGE RESTRICTIONS: CAN'T CARRY A SWORD IN THE CITY!

**DOMINATED**
TINY KNIFE:
HARDLY ANY DAMAGE AND NO REACH.

- RESOURCE ADVANTAGE: YOU ALWAYS KEEP THE DAGGER:
  DURABILITY ONLY BREAKS OTHER WEAPONS.
- NICHE PROTECTION: KNIVES CAN BE USED FOR STEALTH KILLS!

## DOUBLE OR HALVE

Your first go-to for balancing numbers should be doubling or halving them. If you have too many cards in your deck, try using half the number. If you have too few, try twice the number. This is one of the fastest and most reliable ways to approach many balancing issues and in many cases it's all you really need.

Naturally, doubling and halving back and forth won't do you much good; it's the balancing equivalent to running around in circles. But as a first tweak to something that needs balancing, double or halve is probably the best tool there is.

Double or Halve Examples

- Double or halve the expected length of a game session.
- Double or halve the amount of damage of a weapon.
- Double or halve the allowed timing for a double-click in the input system.
- Double or halve how many enemies the player fights in a given encounter.
- Double or halve the amount of points awarded for picking up a coin.
- Double or halve how many cards a player has on hand.
- Double or halve the total number of levels in your game.
- Double or halve the size of a character.
- Double or halve the prices in the in-game shop, and check purchase patterns.
- Double or halve the number of character creation options available.
- Double or halve timer duration before the player loses the game.
- Double or halve how many different endings you have in your story.
- Double or halve how many actions a player gets each turn.
- Double or halve movement speed for the player.
- Double or halve the number of points needed to win.

- Double or halve how big your physical components are.

- Double or halve the value of all the game's collectable treasures.

- Double or halve the number of dialogue alternatives a player can choose from.

- Double or halve the length and/or height of the player's jump.

- Double or halve the number of players who can play at the same time.

- Double or halve the total number of cards in the game.

- Double or halve how many words are allowed per block of player-facing text.

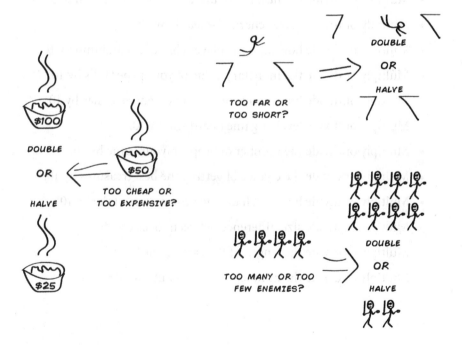

## BY 10

Often when we tweak things, the instinct is to do it just a little. As designers, we get a sense of the difference a small change makes because we are familiar with the game we're working on, and we sometimes mistake that sense of familiarity for a universal impression.

But this may not be enough to make an impression on the people playing or testing the game. They may feel that it's still behaving exactly the same.

A quick guiding principle for when you want *more* impact from a change is therefore to do things in multiples of ten.

Maybe it turns out that your 3-minute game is suddenly a lot more interesting when it plays in 30 minutes; or that what was a 30-minute slog becomes a 3-minute blast.

By 10 Examples

- Multiply or divide game session length by 10.
- Multiply or divide the number of units in your strategy game by 10.
- Multiply or divide player character health by 10.
- Multiply or divide how high the player character can jump by 10.
- Multiply or divide the monetary value of your paper bills by 10.
- Multiply or divide how many zombies a necromancer has by 10.
- Multiply or divide level or game board size by 10.
- Multiply or divide the number of props in your game by 10.
- Multiply or divide the chance of getting the best treasures by 10.
- Multiply or divide how much damage enemies can take by 10.
- Multiply or divide size difference between tokens by 10.
- Multiply or divide the length of the early game by 10.
- Multiply or divide the number of checkpoints by 10.

- Multiply or divide how many dice players roll by 10.
- Multiply or divide the number of dialogue alts by 10.
- Multiply or divide your game's resource costs by 10.
- Multiply or divide how many cards you include by 10.
- Multiply or divide your game's collectable count by 10.
- Multiply or divide how often events happen by 10.
- Multiply or divide player actions per turn by 10.

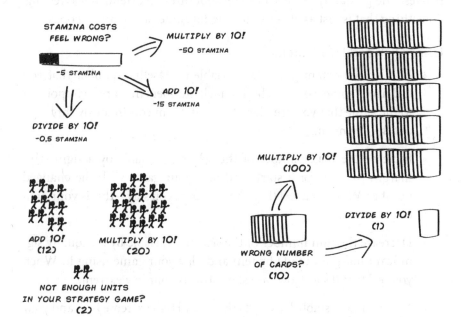

## TEST FOR EXTREMES

An 'extreme' in this context is the highest or lowest possible value that can be used for something in your game. The start and end points of the slider that define the range of values you are considering.

For example, if you find a boss has too much health you set the current value as its max, then you decrease it and try again. When you find the value that's simply too low, you use that value as the low extreme. The old value is the max—the new value is the min. There you have your extremes.

Once you have both extremes, you have a spectrum you can stay within, and simply increasing the min and decreasing the max will let you gradually find the sweet spot.

A good way to test inside this range is to use a random number each playtest and gradually reach said sweet spot through extended playtesting. Something that is just as effective for digital games as for analog ones.

### Using High and Low Extremes

- Find an important gameplay variable or baseline number that you feel needs some work. It's best to pick numbers that are so important to the game that you are likely to tweak them continuously throughout development..

- Increase the max number of the selected variable by a significant margin (by ten, for a start) and play your game with the changed number. When you feel that it's too much, you stay—this is your high extreme.

- Decrease the min number of the selected variable by an equally significant margin (divide by ten) and play your game using it. When you feel that it's too low, you stay—this is your low extreme.

- Now you can establish as Facts that your High extreme is X, and your Low extreme is Y. You will never again go higher than High or lower than Low.

- Things you can use this tool on:

  - **Game end conditions**: Number of points needed to win, boss health, duration before completion, world size, *etc.*

  - **Progression numbers**: Enemy health, value of pickups, experience needed to gain levels, amount of ammo available, total number of cards drawn in a whole play session, *etc.*

  - **Difficulty levels**: The Low can be the player's starting point, while the High is the highest supported difficulty.

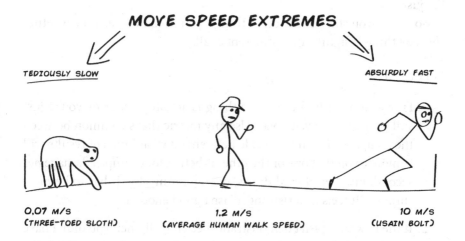

**MOVE SPEED EXTREMES**

TEDIOUSLY SLOW

ABSURDLY FAST

0.07 M/S
(THREE-TOED SLOTH)

1.2 M/S
(AVERAGE HUMAN WALK SPEED)

10 M/S
(USAIN BOLT)

## LIFT THINGS UP

Let's say you have added a new gun to your game. It's a ton of fun to use and players are responding well to it. But you feel it's a bit overpowered. It seems much better than the other guns in the game, or at least more fun to use.

The gut reaction here will be to "nerf" the new gun and make it more on par with the other guns in your game. But before you do, try lifting the others instead. If players respond well to the new gun, they may be on to something, and you should promote whatever they're on to.

However, before you do there is something to consider. The risk when you add something new and find it more enjoyable than the old is that you are in fact running into novelty bias. The new thing is more fun because it's new and feels better because it's new. It's not actually more fun or better, just new.

So before you start lifting other things, you need to determine whether the new thing is significantly different at all.

Lift or Leave?

1. First you must find out if the thing is actually better or you're just suffering from novelty bias. Use any metric that's common between the compared features. Decide beforehand what kinds of results will convince you that one or the other is better, for example, damage per second, number of card draws, or something else. It has to be measurable. "It feels faster/stronger" isn't good enough.

2. If the new thing isn't demonstrably better at all, then you didn't have a problem to begin with; you merely ran into novelty bias. But if the new thing is demonstrably better, consider both of the following strategies:

   a. What would it take to make the other options in your game yield the same results as the new thing?

   b. What would it take to make this new option perform like the other options in your game instead of standing out?

3. Implement the change that sounds most reasonable and also fits into your budget and schedule.

## USE FOILING

Foiling in storytelling and elsewhere is inspired by how jewelers would mount a precious gem over tin foil to bring out its luster. In storytelling, this is often a matter of personality. If the main protagonist is generous, you can "foil" this generosity by adding a greedy or cheap character as a sidekick, supporting character, or villain. This will serve to contrast the generosity of the generous character.

The same principle of having something cheap enhance the visible "glow" of something valuable can be applied in game design.

In any game with treasure of variable rarity, for example, the veritable busloads of useless common items that you haul around serve to foil the rarer items. The psychology of finding the "rare loot" is enhanced by having an unending fountain of worthless loot.

Similarly, defeating hordes of easier enemies serves both to teach the player how to play and as foils for any tougher more complex enemies.

Exfoliation

- **Jumping**: low and less challenging jumps teach you the mechanic and make it feel more interesting to do the harder jumps.

- **Units**: building and controlling many smaller units in a strategy game may make the big ones feel more interesting and unique; "worth" their investment.

- **Weapons**: a smaller or slower weapon will make it feel more interesting to find a bigger or faster one.

- **Speed**: after walking around on foot for a long while, the gains of using a horse or motorcycle will far outweigh the need to groom and refuel.

- **Combos**: after playing common cards to set up your devastating combo, it will feel all the more satisfying to play the finishing rare card.

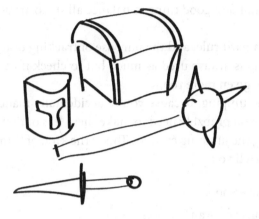

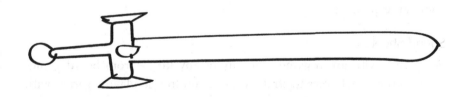

## BALANCE COVERAGE

If you have a wide range of features in your game, or just some ways that certain things can be selected over others, it's a good thing to take a closer look at how they balance out in play.

Let's say that you have six different actions that your player can take. If one of those is used 20 times per session, on average, and another is used 40 times, it could be a good thing to balance all six to around 10 times per session.

This is not a hard rule, and the purpose of tracking usage isn't to make sure everything is always used as much but to check if there are features that need to be given more room.

If no one is jumping, because you've accidentally made all the jumps optional, then you probably need to make them less optional or even consider removing the jumping entirely. This is the kind of thing a usage sheet may be able to tell you.

### Making a Usage Sheet

- List actions you want to track.

- Provide check boxes or circles next to each action.

- Each time an action is used in a play test, or by yourself, you check one box.

### Representation Sheet

An alternative version of a usage sheet is a representation sheet. Define a way to measure representation. One example is the Bechdel Test, where "at least two women who talk to each other about something other than a man" is required to pass the test.

When you have such a definition of the representation you want—whether cultural, social, or something else—you check one box each time your game qualifies.

### Spend Sheet

For games with an in-game economy of any kind—from board games with auction mechanics to strategy games on to role-playing games with vendors buying and selling items—it's important to track the flow of that economy.

The simplest form is a sheet where you list **Money In** and **Money Out**: the economy's sources and sinks. It's just like a usage sheet, but you add the value of virtual currency as a piece of data in the sheet. So rather than just checking a box, it may say +10 gold, +150 gold, –12 gold, *etc.*

This is used to check the health of the in-game economy and, typically, to make sure that there are more sinks than sources so that what a player does with their hard-earned pretend money becomes an interesting choice. In other words: in most kinds of game economies, you want the tally of the sources and sinks to be negative.

## ACTION SHEET

### PRIMARY GUN KILL

### SIDEARM KILL

### MELEE KILL

### STEALTH KILL

### DIALOGUE KILL

## REPRESENTATION

### FEMALE/NON-BINARY

### AFRICAN

### INDONESIAN

### ASIAN

### NATIVE AMERICAN

USE THESE TYPES OF CHECKLISTS TO VERIFY THAT YOUR CLAIMS AND HOPES ARE ACTUALLY TRUE!

## SIMPLIFY YOUR MATH

Even if mathematics may be the universal language of science, its intricacies aren't nearly as intuitive as we may wish they were. No matter how much you think you have already simplified the player-facing math of your game, chances are that it needs to be even simpler.

Even in games where you want visible numbers and in-depth number crunching, it's important to make it accessible. Though some games may simply give you a window that covers the whole screen in numbers, or whole binders of tables and charts, deciding to do so risks alienating parts of your potential player base.

There are two keys to player-facing formulas: **show the data** and **show comparisons**. But you can always work to make both the data and the comparisons more readable.

Fortunately, there are a number of pedagogical shortcuts you can take.

One thing to keep in mind is that the average number of items in short-term human memory is seven plus/minus two (5–9) (sometimes called Miller's Law). This means that the typical player will be able to remember between five and nine things at a given time. For children, this number can be slightly lower. Let's call it five plus/minus two (3–7).

It's no coincidence that many games use three states for boss fights, three lives, and other multiples of three—it's a variable most players, of most ages, can keep in short-term memory.

### Math Considerations Checklist

- **Use graphics**: before showing any numbers, consider using graphical data comparisons instead: arrows, colors, and diagrams.

- **Be consistent**: setting up hard rules for your player-facing data such as "High Numbers are Always Good" or "Negative Numbers are Always Bad" forces you to conform to a communicable standard.

- **Fuzzy numbers**: consider using words that express the numbers. "Near Death" communicates low health faster than "5/100."

- **Addition** is the fastest arithmetic operation. If you want the player to count numbers in their head, make it addition.

- **Higher than** is the most intuitive comparison, and static comparisons are easier than variable ones. If you know that the difficulty is always 20 when you roll dice, you can make the comparison faster.

- **Multiples of five** are the fastest and most intuitive multiplication.

- **Use integers**. In a game where you want to add +0.25, you can always consider multiplying all baseline numbers by four so you can use +1 instead. Whole numbers are much easier than fractions.

- **Use percentages**. If your game still needs fractions, try replacing the multipliers with percentages. x1.1 is less intuitive than +10%.

- If you're still not convinced that you can do away with fractions— make them single- or at most double-digit fractions, and try to apply the other mathematical shortcuts. That is, x1.75 reads better than x1.7481139.

- Make it clear if you are adding multiples or resolving them cumulatively. Some games handle multipliers differently depending on what's being multiplied: this breaks the second rule of being consistent.

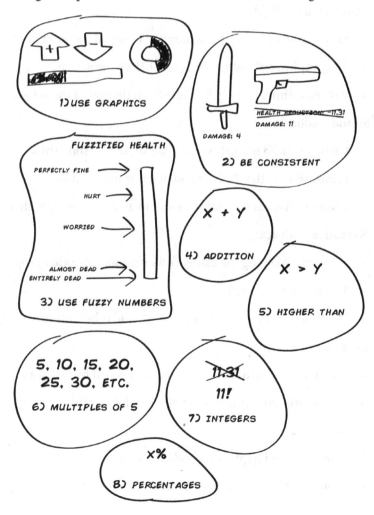

## TWEEN MORE

In animation, an "inbetween" is a drawing that complements the main poses of the action with intermediate drawings. The goal is to generate a gentle curve through the motion.

Say that a character is jumping. The three main poses of this may be the standing idle, the midair launch, and then the superhero landing. Between those three poses, you use inbetweens.

The same principle applies to game design, and in some ways even more so.

This is still a balancing tool simply because it will sometimes be the difference between not understanding what's going on and making your game feel nice to play.

Action Feedback

- **Animation** feedback:

  - **Stop frames**: pausing for a moment to signal a state change.

  - **Telegraphing**: showing the intent before the action.

  - **Returns**: animating back to idle from the end of the action.

- **Sound** feedback:

  - **Cues**: an audio indication that you should do something.

  - **Hints**: sounds that inform you of game information.

  - **Chimes**: plays as a direct response to an action or state change.

- **Narrative** feedback:

  - **Camera**: changing the camera's focus, zoom, or other properties.

  - **Voice-over**: recorded dialogue.

  - **Writing**: text prompts, in-game text, and other forms of copy.

- **Effect** feedback:

  - **Particles**: any visual effects that are spawned by the game.

  - **Highlights**: color, outline, or other visible outlines.

- **Force** feedback:

  - **Vibration and haptics**: for indication or action reinforcement.

  - **Camera shake**: to further enhance visual impact.

- **Dialogue** feedback:

  - **Barks**: single isolated lines signaling game state.

  - **Reinforcement**: lines spoken in response to player interaction.

  - **Repartee**: remarks based on other spoken dialogues.

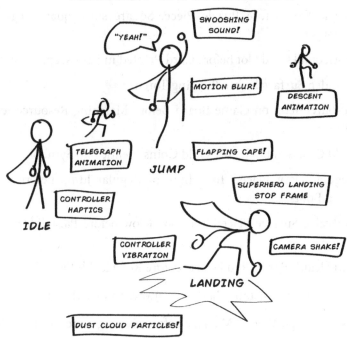

## PUT THE DOOR BEFORE THE KEY

They can be puzzles, special enemies, or specific mechanics. Some situations and mechanics in games require that the player understands the solution before they can know what to look for. This required solution is the key.

It can be a straightforward actual key, like a weirdly shaped object that needs to be slotted into a niche to open a door. But it can also be something more transient, like boots that let you jump higher or a card that must be played before you can open the next envelope in your legacy board game.

But keys without context are almost entirely useless. Finding the sealed envelope in your board game box that says "open when you win your tenth game" and discovering the door that blocks your path and its weirdly shaped slot; when the player discovers these things first, they will understand almost immediately what they need to do.

At the very least, they'll know that they need to do something in order to progress, and they will have some clue of what to look for.

Doors before Keys

- Steel-armored seemingly immortal enemy before Electric Weapon.

- Colored Door before Identically Colored Key.

- Colored Enemies before Colored Weapon Projectiles.

- Puzzle Slot before Puzzle Piece. Square slot, square peg—many variations.

- Horizontal Card Slot before Card Printed in Landscape Orientation.

- Wooden Surface before Burning Torch.

- Resource Icon on Game Board Before Matching Resource Icon on Dice.

- Gold Cost Symbol before Gold Coins Identical to Symbol.

- Regular Door Placed Too High for Regular Jump before Double-Jump Boots.

- Walkable Surface Placed Too Far Below before Paraglider to Glide Down.

- Red Health Bar or Red Hearts before Red Health Pickups.

- A Light in the Distance before Pathways toward the Light.

- "Not Enough Wood" Message before Finding a Tree and a Hatchet.

# CHAPTER 7

# Tuning

T HERE COMES A POINT in your game's development where you can no
longer listen to fans of your work or to playtesters but must start the
process of getting your game ready for the market.

You are likely to go back to balancing or even problem solving from
here a few times before you feel ready enough, but it should only be in
extreme cases and to resolve highly specific isolated issues. Once you start
tuning, you're in the game's last stretch before release. Compare it to "post-
production," if that helps.

The biggest problem in this whole stage is that you may end up having
to alienate some of your true believers, who helped you balance the game.
Still, shifting from balancing with fans to tuning for the market is absolutely essential. Just don't mistake the word "market" for every person on
the planet. As the saying goes, if you try making something for everyone,
you will end up making it for no one.

After you are done tuning you should have the following:

- A first delivery of the finished game.

- A plan for continued support of the game.

- Marketing materials.

- Ideas for potential add-ons, sequels, or patches that you can be ready
  to start working on at short notice if your game is successful.

- Ideas for supporting the game in the long term, in case it's not
  successful.

DOI: 10.1201/9781003332756-8

## REFINE YOUR AUDIENCE

There are three dangers you need to be aware of as you go from balancing to tuning. (Truth be told, there are many more dangers beyond these three, but let's just focus on these three.)

The first is **Creator's Bias**. Thinking that you get it, so players will get it too. You like it, so players will like it too. Putting your Level 4 designer hat on, you have to take a step back and look at the game without your authorship in mind. What it actually achieves versus what you want it to achieve.

The second is **Grognard Capture**—a term invented by Greg Costikyan to explain how many games end up catering to their "hardest core" given enough time and iteration. The vocal minority becomes the people you make the game for rather than the silent majority, sometimes alienating players who could've become fans if the game had fewer barriers of entry.

The third is **Confirmation Bias**. This can take many different forms, but one of the most common ones is to look at the popularity of games that are similar to yours, assume that people will like yours too, and then filter all incoming feedback based on this assumption. In this state of mind, if you think players of *Monopoly* will enjoy your game, and someone says they always play the shoe in that game, you instantly go back to your game to add the shoe.

One way to make sure you don't fall into any of these traps is to refine your view of the target audience more carefully. A process quite similar to an initial pitch, except now you already know what your product is and you can use that information to clarify who you are making the game for.

Target Audience

- Identify your game's hook. The single-sentence thing that will convince people to play (and buy) your game.

- Define your audience pitch: Needs, Approach, Benefits, Competition (NABC):

  - List the **Needs** you are cornering with your game. The types of content or experiences that players may be after.

- List your **Approach** to fulfilling said needs. The thing you're working on.

- List the **Benefits** your approach provides for your customers. Cheaper or faster. Higher quality. Things competitors can't offer at all. More long-term. Cross-media adoption. Specific brand or intellectual property you are offering. Anything and everything.

- List your game's biggest **Competitors**. Other games, but also other game designers or game companies similar to yours.

- Note related interests that tie into your game. Brands customers may like; brands they may dislike. Mainstream culture, specific fandom, platform loyalty, and so on.

- With hook, NABC, and related brands in mind, analyze what kind of target audience you end up with and gather data in any way you can. It may be that this exercise shows you that there are additional groups of players you could reach by making changes to your hook.

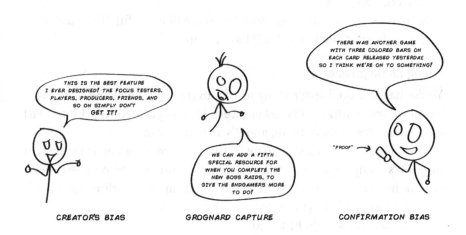

CREATOR'S BIAS          GROGNARD CAPTURE          CONFIRMATION BIAS

## EXTERMINATE YOUR DARLINGS

"Kill your darlings" is an idiom thrown around in creative industries. Games are no different. In fact, killing darlings is a popular shorthand for someone not to be stubborn. (Conveniently, it's almost always someone else's darlings.)

There are actually two different meanings behind this violent exhortation.

The first, to "kill your darlings," is usually used to mean cutting things out that have become important artifacts to someone and kept for no other reason than attachment or habit. It's asking you to cut things out that have passed their sell by dates, or at least to consider cutting them. It's what happens when something has been left in for quite some time, but the reasons for having it have been deprecated.

The other, to "murder your darlings," relates more to cutting things out that are there for the author's benefit and not for the reader's, in writing. It applies the same between developers and gamers. It was first phrased by author Arthur Quiller-Couch, saying "Whenever you feel an impulse to perpetrate a piece of exceptionally fine writing, obey it—wholeheartedly—and delete it before sending your manuscript to press. Murder your darlings."

Murdering your darlings is also personal, but more about getting things out of your system and moving on **right away**. It's not about cutting things out that have become comfortable, but to understand from the start that they're not necessary.

Similar but different tools. Both are incredibly useful. The more darlings you murder, the fewer you'll have to kill.

### Killing Darling Features

You've had this double-sprinting feature in the game since the start, but it has never quite worked. Players get stuck in level geometry, sprint too fast for the enemies to shoot them, and it's all just a bit messy.

The main reason it's still there is that the programmer who made it insists it's going to work at a later date and volunteers to do overtime to get it done. But it's still not done. It's the programmer's darling, sure, but it doesn't actually add anything to the game.

Such a darling should be killed.

### Murdering Darling Features

It is the same double-sprinting feature, but now we rewind the tape back to its conception—all the way back to the ancient days of ideation and exploration.

You feel terribly clever about adding it, since the regular sprint seems to be a bit slow. But you realize the moment you start exploring that it's not worth it because there may be broader issues introduced into the game by moving so fast. You play around with it for a brief bit in exploration, then you cut it out and move on.

You just murdered your darling.

## PUT THE COOL THING FIRST

Data on completion rates for single-player games are grim. Most players who start playing single-player games never finish them, and only around 25%–30% of players who begin playing will ever reach the end (looking at Steam achievement rates for a range of single-player games).

The same goes for many kinds of games, where players get stuck in the interface's intricacies, feel like there's too many components or rules that are too dense, and so on. Many in the *Advanced Squad Leader* community joke that no one has ever finished a whole session of its massive historical scenarios, because it's usually evident who will win quite early on, and no one wants to go through the motions just because they should technically do so. Instead, the losing side will forfeit the match mid-way through.

With an increasing number of platforms providing free games, initial player commitment is also getting smaller and the window of opportunity for a game to convince someone to play it shrinks accordingly.

This makes it important for your game to get to its coolest parts quickly. The hard part is to know which parts are the coolest parts, and to admit to yourself that the parts that aren't the coolest parts should be given less attention.

### What Is the Cool Thing?

- **Not the modal prompt**: Fullscreen prompts that are unskippable, timed, or require that the player reads more than a single sentence of text.

- **Not the rulebook**: Having to read a large chunk of a rulebook before getting to the game is a big turnoff for many players. Providing how to play-videos, quick start rules, visual guides, and other means to get into the game faster will all help the game's appeal.

- **Not the exposition**: The player is highly unlikely to care about anything beyond context and calls to action when starting a new game. If you spend too much time writing players on the nose, there's a risk that you may lose some of them. Parcel out the narrative and context, and let players do things.

- **Not the tutorial**: If you are tutorializing everything, chances are you will bore your players. If they are playing a first-person shooter, you probably don't need to explain how they move or aim. The same thing is observed with the basic use of cards and shuffling. Make any extensive tutorials opt-in instead of opt-out.

- **Not the why.** Unlike much popular fiction, the why is rarely that important to players. Where a movie character may have to lose their kid or spouse to get into action mode, players will start in action mode by merely starting the game. If you want to provide a solid why, do so after the player has had a chance to try out the cool stuff they will get to do, not before.

- **Not the ads.** If your game has ads of any kind—particularly ones that pause the game—you should be careful to let your players play before you show them any ads. Downloading and launching a game only to be greeted by an unskippable ad is a surefire turnoff (and possibly uninstall).

## PUT THE COOL
## THING FIRST!

*SO YOU MEAN TO TELL ME THAT 10% OF PEOPLE WHO BUY A GAME, NEVER ACTUALLY PLAY IT?!*

### ESTIMATED PLAYER
### RETENTION*

| | |
|---|---|
| 100% | MOMENT OF PURCHASE |
| 90% | UNBOXING/MENU SPLASH |
| 80% | GAME START/LEARNING PHASE |
| 70% | POST-LEARNING PHASE |
| 60% | MID-GAME |
| 50% | LATE GAME |
| 40% | FINAL PHASE |
| 30% | END OF GAME |
| 20% | EARLY ENDGAME/PACKING UP |
| 10% | MID-ENDGAME |
| <10% | LATE ENDGAME |

*NOPE. I MEAN TO TELL YOU THAT THIS IS PROBABLY A **GENEROUS** ESTIMATE...*

*BASED ON STEAM ACHIEVEMENT DATA
FROM A SAMPLING OF AROUND 250 SINGLE-PLAYER GAMES.

## REMOVE UNINFORMED CHOICES

An uninformed choice is a choice where the player doesn't yet know the difference between available options. Games that use some form of character creation or have you select a faction in the early game are some examples of choices that will be uninformed when someone plays the game for the first time.

Once you get used to the game and how it works, this choice will be important, and you can make it in an informed way that affects how you play. But the first time you play, you have no way of knowing what +15% Science or an extra resource card even means.

Removing choices like this from the early game allows players to make more informed choices later on, and to get into the early game faster. You don't have to remove the character creation or special card abilities entirely—just move them to a stage in the game where the options require less explanation.

This is also where many of the classic game design tropes come from. If you can pick one of three established character classes that are the same in this game as in many other games, this seemingly provides a shortcut. But it also makes it a requirement to be immersed in the overall gaming culture where those choices mean something. For anyone who is unfamiliar with the tropes, the choice will be just as uninformed as any other uninformed choice.

### Identifying Uninformed Choices

If the answer to any of the following checklist questions is "no," chances are that you are asking the player to make an uninformed choice:

- Will the choice make only a cosmetic difference? (Selecting a skin, picking a color, *etc.*)

- Has the player interacted with all of the features that are affected by the choice before the choice is made?

- Are the potential consequences of each available option known to the player before the choice is made?

- Will the choice have a significant noticeable outcome for the player?

- Are the consequences of the choice immediate?

- If the consequences are not immediate, will there be a clear callback to the choice once the consequences do occur?

- If the player hasn't interacted with the features, is there an effective shorthand that you can use to introduce the choices anyway? (Think of roles, character classes, and other stereotypes that may be applicable to your game.)

- Is the shorthand from the previous question something that the player can be expected to know intuitively, without having to be immersed in any specific culture, hobby, or previous game release?

- If there is an opportunity cost—for example a cost in resources or the loss of future options in a different choice—is the meaning of that cost made clear to the player before they have to make the choice?

## ALLOW CUSTOMIZATION

Playing a game their way has always been an important part of many gamers' identities, and today more than ever.

When people started playing *Quake* in the mid-1990s, most players played with just the keyboard. The first-person control scheme established by id Software's earlier game—*Doom*—was that you used the arrow keys to move and turn, the control (CTRL) key to fire your weapon, and the space bar to open doors. But *Doom* also had a tip in its manual. "When you're comfortable playing the game, try using the keyboard and the mouse simultaneously." Knowing how first-person shooters are played on PC today, this is more than a little nostalgic, but the discussion among gamers at the time was whether you stuck to the old way or embraced "using the keyboard and the mouse simultaneously."

But customization goes far beyond the choice of whether to stick to the tried and true or try the new way. With solid customization options you can turn people who would otherwise be completely unable to play your game into potential players. Sometimes the changes you need to implement are trivial; at other times the changes may require a lot of technical work or even that you must rebuild your game, add extra content, or reprint components.

Think of customization taken to its logical extreme: if someone wants to play your first-person shooter with just one hand, or using a surfboard peripheral, in the best of worlds it would be possible to accommodate them.

Example Customization

- Ability to skip particularly challenging or overwhelming segments.
- Allowing players to undo/redo actions before committing.
- Customization of game rules (gravity, attempt counts, *etc.*), and game data (move speeds, card counts, *etc.*).
- Left- and right-handed base controller layouts.
- Single-hand controller layout options.
- Automation of repetitive actions.
- Detailed button layout customization, including support for custom hardware controllers.
- Changing interactions between Press, Hold, and Toggle.
- Changing for how long a button must be held down, if it must be held.

- Text size, color, and font selection.
- Text placement on-screen.
- Capping how much text appears at any one time.
- Subtitling; for dialogue, but also prompts for the hearing impaired.
- Color options for all visible elements.
- Where you can choose colors, make it possible to choose patterns.
- Make it possible to order cards printed with Braille.
- Optional highlights, with choice of colors.
- Turning animation on or off.
- Toggling triggering or traumatizing content on/off.

## OFFEND ON PURPOSE

Sometimes the story you want to tell or the feature you want to include is an offensive one. It may be violent, sexual, religious, or politically controversial in nature. It may be inhuman or horrific—many many games portray graphic violence, for example.

When you make a game, and you decide to have offensive content in that game, you will be responsible for making that decision and for any outrage or controversy it may cause.

But the fact is that you may also have something in your game that is extremely offensive to someone from a particular background or with some particular conviction, and you don't even know that it's offensive. You just thought it was a "cool" thing to have and never thought twice about it.

Trouble is—you must know. It's your job to know. You must introduce your game to people who could have something to say about it, no matter how their views may seem to you or your creative sensibilities.

If you offend someone, you must be doing so on purpose and make sure you are informed enough to answer for it. You must have good reasons for it that aren't just some variations of doing what you please because you can, or accidentally offending because you didn't know better. None of that is good enough.

Sometimes being offensive is the whole point. Just make sure that you know whether your game is offensive before it offends anyone and be prepared to defend your choices when it does. Also respect that not everyone will agree with your choice.

### Localization

Translating a game to a new language is referred to as localization. On the surface, this means switching out written words for the words of another language. But the meaning of a word or sentence doesn't always translate well.

Sometimes language is used more as decoration or world-building—for example game world signage—but this needs to be localized the same as any other language used in your game.

If you localize your game, make sure that each supported translation is thoroughly vetted by native speakers of the particular language.

### Culturalization

Analyzing a game through a cultural lens is sometimes referred to as culturalization. This is much harder than localization and requires that you have access to people who can inform you of what you should be doing. There are paid experts who offer such services, but even just asking someone you know who has a better understanding of the culture in question will make you more informed.

Some countries will have rules on what you are allowed to depict. Graphical violence may cause restrictions on where you can offer your game for sale, for example.

Other countries may have cultural or religious limitations or may want you to remove certain stereotypes from your game.

Other cultural symbols can be so sacred or culturally specific that their depiction is deemed appropriation if they are included. You must be aware of them.

## IF YOU OFFEND,
## DO SO ON PURPOSE.

## PUT IT ELSEWHERE

Consider how your game would work on a smartphone, on game consoles, as a board game, a card game, cosplay, a novel, or a movie. This exercise helps you identify the core more easily and helps you understand what makes a brand work as opposed to just a game.

This may seem like it's the domain of marketing and not game design, but it's important for you as a game designer to be aware of more than the features and gameplay and to make decisions that help facilitate marketing.

Some decisions will have to be made earlier. You can't make a complex character more plushable once you reach tuning, for example. But thinking of your game as a product and how it could be viewed more as a mainstream phenomenon and less as "just a game" is a great exercise at this stage.

If your game is successful, people may want to engage with your ideas in more ways than by playing the game. If you've already put it elsewhere in your head, you will be better prepared.

Moving It Elsewhere

- **Relatable**: Superheroes may be superheroes, but it's no coincidence that some of the most popular ones are teenagers having teenage problems while saving the world. It intersects with the audience the authors were writing for. Making the game's subject matter closer to its audience, so that the struggles and conflicts can be related to on an emotional level makes it relatable.

- **Agreeable**: Making sure that any blood, gore, nudity, and other instances of potentially less agreeable content is contrasted and doesn't dominate the whole product. Some games of course thrive on the opposite, but many highly successful gaming franchises are fundamentally agreeable.

- **Plushable**: Making characters, vehicles, and other central objects have features and color schemes that are distinguishable and can be caricatured to the point that you can make plush toys out of them and still recognize them for what they are.

- **Tattooable**: Making your iconography easy to draw with single lines and in black and white, making them attractive as tattoos, stickers, or other shorthand symbols.

- **Memeable**: Writing language and presenting animation that can be repeated easily and provide contextual meaning without further explanation. May even include bugs or developer-facing features, if you have access to a community that enjoys the sharing of such things.

- **Cosplayable**: Making costume silhouettes that are striking and recognizable, but also considering what kinds of materials and patterns you include so that any potential costumes are not too exotic or hard for a cosplayer to produce.

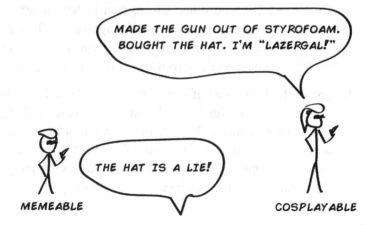

## MAKE IT FUN TO WATCH

Not all games are interesting to watch. Some games are animated too fast or too jittery to make for satisfying viewing, while other games are too slow or esoteric. Turning a game that's fun to play into entertainment for viewers is tricky, but there are some things you can consider.

Imagine being a writer that has 5 minutes between ads to tell a story and knows that some viewers may drop in or out between those ads to check out your show. The show has to be entertaining both for the continuously viewing die hard fanatic and for the casual viewer who happens to turn on the TV at a specific time.

The same dynamic exists for Twitch, YouTube, and the many other current ways people can engage with video content.

You want these streamers to play your game and show it to potential players in the process. To make this happen, you must make your game fun to watch.

### Making Something Fun to Watch

- **Communicate goals**: Viewers must be able to understand what's happening, if it's going well for the person playing or not, and what to look out for.

- **Smooth motion**: Much of our intuition with game design is based on how something feels, particularly in the digital space. Unfortunately, many of the quick and rapid cuts that we do as abbreviated forms of animations look jittery and jarring when you watch someone else play. To make a game fun to watch, this may need to be smoother.

- **Communicate what's happening**: Using stop frames, explanations, on-screen prompts, and other information to tell viewers what is happening in a visual way is extremely important. Where a player may pick up on discrete visual cues and controller haptics, a viewer will only have what's on the screen and in their ears to go on.

- **Empower the influencer**: If you want your game to be played, not only must you make it fun to watch, but you must also make the person playing your game look good. They're not in it to promote your game but to entertain their fans. Find influencers that play games like the one you are making and ask them what makes a game particularly entertaining for their audience. They're the experts.

- **Name the game**: Display the game's logo repeatedly. In pause menus, on reward screens, on progression screens—anywhere you can. If someone stumbled in by chance, they shouldn't have to wonder what game it is.

- **Use repetition**: The same as for the name, you need to remind players who the characters are, what the goals are, and so on, in the game.

- **Integrate engagement**: If you have the resources, make it possible for stream viewers to customize content, suggest solutions, or otherwise engage directly with the game while it is played by an influencer.

- **Support streaming**: Provide toggles to turn off potentially copyrighted music. Make it possible to play the game in a windowed borderless mode. Make sure the game board isn't too glossy, causing camera glare. There are many things you can do to facilitate your game's "streamability."

## HOW GAMES MAY SOUND TO OUTSIDERS

### AND WHAT YOU MUST DEAL WITH TO MAKE IT FUN TO WATCH!

## THINK LIKE A PLAYER

By this time in a game project, you're so deep into the inner workings of your game that it can be hard to see the game the way your players will see it when they see it for the first time.

The difference in perspective between a developer and a player can be looked at as a division of three things we already mentioned: Mechanics, Dynamics, and Aesthetics.

As a game designer, you design the mechanics in the hope that you generate interesting dynamics, and aesthetics are then the player-facing representation of what you have made.

Players will then approach it the exact opposite way. They will first approach the aesthetics, and then engage with the dynamics of play, and finally they may learn about the mechanics behind it all if they put enough time into it.

We'll use the character Indiana Jones as a parallel. Regardless of whether you like the films or the character or not, most of you will be familiar with the fedora-sporting archaeologist. If a new film is announced, it'll tout this pulpy hero immediately—hey, look, it's that hero you know and love; come see the new film!

But for the first film, *Raiders of the Lost Ark*, that wasn't possible. No one was yet familiar with the "Mechanics" of the character or even the name Indiana Jones. Instead, the trailer focused on the mystery of the Ark of the Covenant—the artifact sought after in the film—and doesn't sell you on the character at all except by showing action and mystery. The trailer focused on the "Aesthetic" of Indiana Jones.

This is exactly what it means to think like a player. Finding the aesthetic—the mystery—that will make your players want to play your game.

### Mystery and Activities

Have play testers and other external parties look at the assets for your game and focus on whether there is a **mystery** pulling them in and what **activities** they expect.

- **Marketing material**: even before people partake in the actual game, they are likely to see marketing material. Start from there and look at the effect of which character you choose to show and which key art you publish first. Different mysteries; different promises. Note what they pick up on.

- **The game's title, including any subtitles**: the name is very important for what people will come to expect. If it's a sequel or brand tie-in, this will be different from your own original title, but it still matters.

- **The game's genre**: if you explain the game in terms of game genres— action role-playing game, first-person shooter, worker placement, *etc.*—you need to ask about the implications and how different testers interpret these terms. It's quite common that what a game designer thinks it means is different from what players actually expect.

- **The box art**: if your game has a box—physical or virtual—the art it presents will often come to represent the whole game.

- **Publishing pages and store fronts**: if you look past the narrative components you may know, consider what actions are implied by this art.

- **Game start**: when you boot the game to its very first screen, or unpack the components, this may reinforce the promises made or it may not.

- **Gameplay**: once the player has gone through the whole circus of learning about and buying your game—the biggest question is if they consider the promises met. If they don't, you have failed to think enough like a player.

REMEMBER THAT YOU COME
FROM DIFFERENT PERSPECTIVES!

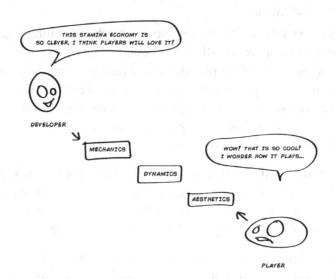

## MEET PLAYER INTENTIONS

When someone starts playing your game, they will come in with expectations that will in turn lead to intentions on their part. If the game then fails to match said intentions, this may cause frustration.

Even if the fanatics of whichever genre you are making your game in may immediately get what you are doing, actively working to make player intent match expectations for all players is fundamental to any successful game product.

Think about the classic question that you can trick kids with: what is heavier, one kg of lead or one kg of feathers? They weigh the same, of course, but that's not what our intuition will try to tell us.

In game design, it's often a good idea to go with our intuition. Steel sinks in water. Wood burns. Jumping across this gap allows me to reach the other side. Turning off my jet engine will make me fall.

In a realistic simulation, some of these examples wouldn't be deterministic at all. A high enough force or small enough mass means that you will keep going up for some time even after you turn off your jet engine. Similarly, a seemingly flammable log may be invisibly damp and not catch fire.

This is what meeting player intent is all about—figure out what the player is trying to achieve and let them achieve it.

If you have cases in your game where this is simply not doable, then you should be as explicit with those exceptions as you possibly can. Or if you are indeed making a simulation—then you have different goals than appealing to intent.

### Accommodate Intent

- **Action *vs* intent**: Sometimes, especially while learning a game, we may do a thing we actually didn't intend. Maybe jump when we were supposed to crouch or play the wrong card from our hand when we couldn't actually afford playing it. In cases like these, the game may need to allow either returning to the previous state, undoing what we just did, or providing enough margin for a few mistakes to be okay without ruining the experience.

- **Context sensitivity**: One way to clarify where your intentions match your options is to make it context sensitive. When you stand next to the ledge, a button prompt appears on-screen that says "Climb," or maybe there is a dab of yellow paint clearly visible where you can climb.

- **"Close Enough" design**: Many games provide assistive features to make you feel great about playing even when the detailed simulation knows that you actually failed. Examples are grabbing a ledge even though you missed it by a short distance, softly tracking the target you are aiming at in your first-person shooter or tracking the player's Jump input even a few frames after your visual character may have walked off a ledge (a "coyote jump," for Wile E. Coyote's tendency to run off ledges before realizing he should fall).

- **Invisible walls**: Adding artificial constraints, such as invisible walls that block players from entering a certain area, is best avoided. It may have to be your solution of last resort, but you should try every thinkable other solution before you add that invisible wall. If there is no intuitive way to understand that your intention to explore will be blocked, it's almost guaranteed frustration.

**COMPARE THIS:**

NO! I'VE TRIED FIFTY-EIGHT TIMES TO JUMP THIS GAP NOW..

DAMNIT! GAME'S LAGGING. I KNOW I HIT THAT ZOMBIE!

**TO MEETING PLAYER INTENT:**

"COYOTE JUMP"

GRABBING THE LEDGE WHEN YOU MISSED BY JUST A LITTLE

+50 POINTS!

"CLOSE ENOUGH" SCORES A HIT

# References

Costikyan, G. 2013. *Uncertainty in Games*. Cambridge, MA: The MIT Press.

Dille, F. and Zuur Platten, J. 2007. *The Ultimate Guide to Video Game Writing and Design*. Hollywood, CA: Lone Eagle.

Hecker, C. 2006. "Advanced Prototyping," *Game Developers Conference, 2006*. Available at: https://www.chrishecker.com/Advanced_Prototyping.

Hunicke, R., LeBlanc, M., and Zubeck, R. 2004. MDA: A Formal Approach to Game Design and Game Research. Available at: https://users.cs.northwestern.edu/~hunicke/MDA.pdf.

Lovell, N. 2019. *The Pyramid of Game Design*. Boca Raton, FL: CRC Press.

Quiller-Couch, A. 2006. On the Art of Writing. Available in the public domain at: https://www.gutenberg.org/ebooks/17470.

Romero, B. and Schreiber, I. 2017. Challenges for Game Designers.

Sellers, M. 2018. *Advanced Game Design: A Systems Approach*. Boston, MA: Pearson Addison-Wesley.

Skinner, B.F. 1953. *Science and Human Behavior*. Glencoe, IL: The Free Press.

Sorkin, A. 2016. "Aaron Sorkin Teaches Screenwriting." Available at: https://www.masterclass.com/classes/aaron-sorkin-teaches-screenwriting.

Swift, K. and Wolpaw, E. 2008. "Integrating Narrative into Game Design: A Portal Post-Mortem," *Game Developers Conference, 2008*. Available at: https://www.youtube.com/watch?v=c2YRVWZupwo.

Valve, Steam return policy, 2023. "Valve Will, upon Request via help.steampowered.com, Issue a Refund for Any Title That Is Requested within 14 Days of Purchase and Has Been Played for Less Than 2 hours (This Includes Online, Offline and Shared Library Playtime)." Available at: https://help.steampowered.com/en/faqs/view/5FDE-BA65-ACCE-A411.

Wolpaw, E. 2000. "Crate Review System." Available at: https://www.oldmanmurray.com/features/39.html.

## LUDOGRAPHY

Blizzard Entertainment. 1998. *StarCraft*. Video game. Blizzard Entertainment.

Bohemia Interactive. 2013. *Arma 3*. Video game. Bohemia Interactive.

Bungie. 2017. *Destiny 2*. Video game. Activision and Bungie.

Chvátil, V. 2011. *Mage Knight Board Game*. Board game. WizKids, Asmodee, etc.

Darrow, C. and Magie, L. 1935. *Monopoly*. Board game. Hasbro, Parker Brothers, etc.

Dennaton Games. 2012. *Hotline Miami*. Video game. Devolver Digital.

DICE. 2018. *Battlefield V*. Video game. Electronic Arts.

Epic Games. 2018. *Fortnite Creative*. Video game. Epic Games.

Firaxis Games. 2016. *Civilization VI*. Video game. 2K and Aspyr Media.

FromSoftware. 2011. *Dark Souls*. Video game. Bandai Namco Entertainment and FromSoftware.

Garfield, R. 1993. *Magic: The Gathering*. Card game. Wizards of the Coast.

Greenwood, D. 1985. *Advanced Squad Leader*. Board game. Avalon Hill and Multi-Man Publishing.

Gygax, G. and Arneson, D. 1974. *Dungeons & Dragons*. Role-playing game. TSR, Wizards of the Coast.

id Software. 1993. *DOOM*. Video game. id Software.

id Software. 1996. *Quake*. Video game. GT Interactive, Activision, Electronic Arts, etc.

Infinity Ward. 2003. *Call of Duty*. Video game. Activision.

Insomniac Games. 2018. *Marvel's Spider-Man*. Video game. Sony Interactive Entertainment.

IO Interactive. 2000. *Hitman: Codename 47*. Video game. Eidos Interactive.

King. 2012. *Candy Crush Saga*. Video game. King.

Looking Glass Studios. 1998. *Thief: The Dark Project*. Video game. Eidos Interactive.

Vaccarino, D. 2008. *Dominion*. Card game. Rio Grande Games.

Valve. 2008. *Portal*. Video game. Valve and Microsoft Game Studios.

# Index

Printed in the United States
by Baker & Taylor Publisher Services